ENCOUNTERING URBAN PLACES

Re-materialising Cultural Geography

Dr Mark Boyle, Department of Geography, University of Strathclyde, UK and
Professor Donald Mitchell, Maxwell School, Syracuse University, USA

Nearly 25 years has elapsed since Peter Jackson's seminal call to integrate cultural geography back into the heart of social geography. During this time, a wealth of research has been published which has improved our understanding of how culture both plays a part in and - in turn - is shaped by social relations based on class, gender, race, ethnicity, nationality, disability, age, sexuality and so on. In spite of the achievements of this mountain of scholarship, the task of grounding culture in its proper social contexts remains in its infancy. This series therefore seeks to promote the continued significance of exploring the dialectical relations which exist between culture, social relations and space and place. Its overall aim is to make a contribution to the consolidation, development and promotion of the ongoing project of re-materialising cultural geography.

The series will publish outstanding original research monographs and edited collections which make strong and clear contributions to the furtherance of the re-materialisation agenda. Work which foregrounds the role of culture in shaping relations of domination and resistance will be particularly welcomed. Both theoretically reflexive contributions charting the progress and prospects of the agenda, and theoretically informed case studies will be sought:

1) the re-materialising agenda - progress and prospects: including the location of the agenda within the broader development of human geography; reflexive accounts of the main achievements to date; outstanding research agendas yet to be explored; methodological innovations and new approaches to field work; and responses to the challenges posed by non-representational theory and theories of performativity.

2) Theoretically informed case studies within the tradition: including work on new links between culutre, capital and social exclusion; changing concepts of masculinity and femininity; nationalism, cosmopoloitanism, colonial and post-colonial identities, diaspora and hybridity; the rescaling of territorial identities, the new regionalism and localism, and the rise of supranational political bodies; sexuality and space; disability and the production of and navigation around the built environment.

Encountering Urban Places

Visual and Material Performances
in the City

Edited by

LARS FRERS AND LARS MEIER
Darmstadt University of Technology, Germany

ASHGATE

Published by
Ashgate Publishing Limited
Gower House
Croft Road
Aldershot
Hampshire GU11 3HR
England

Ashgate Publishing Company
Suite 420
101 Cherry Street
Burlington, VT 05401-4405
USA

Ashgate website: http://www.ashgate.com

British Library Cataloguing in Publication Data

Encountering urban places : visual and material
    performances in the city. - (Re-materialising cultural
    geography)
    1. Sociology, Urban
    I. Frers, Lars II. Meier, Lars
    307.7'6

Library of Congress Cataloging-in-Publication Data

Encountering urban places : visual and material performances in the city / edited by Lars Frers and Lars Meier.
        p. cm. -- (Re-materialising cultural geography)
    Includes index.
    ISBN: 978-0-7546-4929-8
    1. Cities and towns--Study and teaching. 2. Public spaces--Social aspects. 3. Spatial behavior. 4. Group identity. 5. Aesthetics. I. Frers, Lars. II. Meier, Lars.

    HT109.E53 2006
    307.76--dc22

                                                2006021151

ISBN: 978-0-7546-4929-8

Printed and bound in Great Britain by Antony Rowe Ltd, Chippenham, Wiltshire.

Contents

List of Figures

List of Contributors

Deniz Altay is a Ph.D. candidate in the City and Regional Planning program, Middle East Technical University and works as an urban professional, Altay&Altay Architecture Office. She is also researching everyday life and practices in the city. She has written articles on marginal spaces and transgression of architecture (with Can Altay). She also collaborated with Can Altay in the installations 'Active Unemployment: Vending Stands And Hawker Stalls' (Kunsthaus, Dresden; 2005) and 'Minibar Non-Stop' in (Platform, İstanbul, 2003).

Lars Frers is lecturer in sociology and was member of the post-graduate college 'Technology and Society' at Darmstadt University of Technology. He is co-editor of *Negotiating Urban Conflicts* (Transcript 2006) and publishes most of his work on the world wide web. His main research, often relying on video recordings, establishes connections between space and materiality, technology, the body, and social control. Phenomenology and ethnomethodology guide his research and he is also involved in classical social theory from Ibn Khaldun to Karl Marx.

Jerome Krase is professor emeritus and Murray Koppelman Professor for Sociology at Brooklyn College (CUNY). His research focus is on spatial semiotics and visual sociology. Representative books include: *Race and Ethnicity in Urban Areas* (co-editor Ray Hutchinson, Elsevier 2006); *Race and Ethnicity in New York City* (co-editor Ray Hutchinson, Elsevier 2004); *Italian Americans in a Multicultural Society* (co-editor J.N. DeSena, 1994); *Ethnicity and Machine Politics* (with C. LaCerra, 1992); *Self and Community in the City* (1982).

Helen Liggett is a professor in the Levin College of Urban Affairs, Cleveland State University, and a street photographer and urban theorist who works in the art and politics of urban space. She is author of *Urban Encounters* and co-editor of *Spatial Practices* (with David Perry). Her work has been exhibited at MOCA, Cleveland, Campbell Gallery, and Here-Here Gallery, among others. She exhibited photographic installations at the Harare International Festival of the Arts in Zimbabwe and participated in the *Art in Embassies Program,* United States State Department.

Zeuler R.M.A. Lima is assistant professor of architecture at Washington University in Saint Louis, USA, and has also taught at the Universities of Michigan, Columbia, and São Paulo. He has published articles on twentieth-century urbanism and architecture in several countries and is currently writing a book about Italian-Brazilian architect Lina Bo Bardi.

Martina Löw is a professor at Darmstadt University of Technology. She performs research on the sociology of space and cities, and in gender studies. Her publications include *Raumsoziologie* (Suhrkamp 2001, now in its 4th edition) and 'The Social Construction of Space and Gender' in *European Journal of Women's Studies* (2006).

Lars Meier is a geographer and sociologist. He was member of the post-graduate college 'Technology and Society' and lecturer in sociology at the Darmstadt, and is a graduated of the universities of Trier and Göttingen. He is co-editor of *Negotiating Urban Conflicts* (Transcript 2006). His research focus is on urban studies, cultural geography, ethnography, and on migration and globalization theory. Currently, he is performing an ethnographic study of expatriate German bankers in their everyday life in urban places in London and Singapore.

Vera M. Pallamin is associate professor of architecture at Universidade de São Paulo, Brazil, with a degree in philosophy. She has published a book and several articles on contemporary public art and urban public spaces and is currently developing research on the relationship between aesthetics and politics.

Łukasz Stanek is from Kraków, Poland. After his studies in Kraków, Weimar, and Münster, he graduated in architecture and in philosophy. He has been working in architectural studios in Germany, Italy, and the Netherlands. A research scholarship took him to the ETH Zürich, and currently he is a doctoral candidate at the Technical University Delft, Department of Architecture Theory. His forthcoming publications include contributions to volumes on new interpretations of Lefebvre's theory of space (Routledge, forthcoming, 2007) and on cities in socialism (Technical University Berlin, forthcoming, 2006).

Katharine S. Willis is from London. Her work over the last ten years has focused on exploring ways in which we interact with our spatial surroundings, and in particular approaches to understanding how we can create legible environments. These projects investigate wayfinding, identity, and the transformative possibilities of mobile and wireless technologies. Katharine trained as an architect and is currently a researcher in the MEDIACITY project at the Bauhaus University of Weimar in Germany.

Preface

Encounters were the source from which this volume developed. In the spring of 2003 we found ourselves at the same academic place, as scholarship holders in the post-graduate college 'Technology and Society', and as participants in the developing research collective on urban studies at the University of Technology Darmstadt. Being motivated to cooperate on this volume is one of the many pleasant outcomes of the stimulating and supporting academic atmosphere that we experienced there and that is still a welcome part of our academic life.

This book is a follow-up to the 2005 conference 'Technological and Aesthetic (Trans)Formations of Society' in Darmstadt, the concluding conference of the post-graduate college. The many kind encounters and exchanges with the presenters, their insightful academic work, and the close relation of the presentations to each other made it obvious that we should try to form a book out of the panel 'Urban Spaces and Private Quarters' that we hosted at this conference.

For preparing and executing the conference our sincere thanks go to the whole conference team, especially to Anne Batsche for her relentless and thorough coordination work. Sybille Frank has been an outstanding chair for our panel.

In preparing this book we are very grateful to have had Valerie Rose as an always encouraging and helpful editor. We also send our thanks to Donna Hamer and Neil Jordan from Ashgate for their close cooperation. We have enjoyed working with the contributors to this volume tremendously and are proud of being able to offer our readers so many exciting and visually rich chapters.

Lars Frers and Lars Meier
Berlin and Göttingen,
May 2006

Acknowledgements

The authors and publishers are thankful for having permission to reproduce the following material:

Figures 9.1 and 9.2 Socland exhibition in Nowa Huta 2001, *Source*: Fundacja Socland, Muzeum Komunizmu.

Figure 9.3 The foam copy of the Lenin monument in the Aleja Róz in Nowa Huta, *Source*: Anna Kaczmarz, Dziennik Polski.

Figures 9.4 and 9.5 'Nowa Huta – the experience', directed by Bruno Lajara 2004, *Source*: Ryszard Kornecki, Teatr Stary w Krakowie.

Figure 9.6 'I lived here', spectacle in Łaźnia Nowa 2004, *Source*: Krescenty Głazik.

Chapter 1

Encountering Urban Places – Visual and Material Performances in the City

Lars Frers and Lars Meier

(Social) space is a (social) product. (Lefebvre 1991, 26)

Walking along a street in the city, we encounter countless signs, sounds, smells, materialities, people, and movements. Encountering places in everyday life, one engages the place with all senses, interacting with others, with the materiality, and with the atmosphere of the place. By moving these encounters with urban places into the focus of attention, we are coming to terms with the materiality and aesthetics of the place, the body, the perception, and the representations of the place.

Encountering representations

Encounters are produced in contests about the meanings and about the concrete structure of places. We are bringing specific meanings into places and into social groups. These meanings are not set and static; they are socially constructed. Encounters are part of this process of constructing meanings. In these encounters, meanings are impressed on places and social groups in a particular way. How and what is being impressed in these concrete encounters is to a significant degree preconfigured – we don't encounter human beings for themselves, we are encountering people that we differentiate by identities that we ascribe to them. In consequence, in encountering people on the street one is also encountering specific identities like gender, ethnicity or class/milieu on first sight. The perception of the other is accompanied by specific expectations, which we are assigning in our gaze. Ascribing specific meanings to identities, the concrete encounter is regulated by these ascriptions. Simultaneously, however, the identities are produced, reproduced, or modified in these encounters.

Representations of places are everywhere – in maps, photos, novels, advertising, talks, metaphors, or souvenirs – ordering these places and ascribing specific meanings to them. In encountering urban places, one brings these meanings to them; meanings that have been produced as a consequence of the representations of them (Said 1978; Duncan and Ley 1993; Barnes and Duncan 1992; Shields 1996). Thinking of a specific place therefore means thinking of the place in specific images such as modern, dangerous, friendly, dynamic, exotic, or lively. The ascription of meanings to social groups and to urban places directs activities in encounters with these groups and places. Analyzing localized encounters, one analyzes in turn the social and spatial construction of meanings and the powerful outcomes of the contestation of meanings in everyday activity. The translation of meaning into practice and the production of meaning through practices are thus casting urban encounters into their specific shape. Representations of space also have a more general impact on the space of the city, on its places and its encounters: realizing abstract conceptualizations of space – be they based in geometric or military, economic or aesthetic considerations – without regard to the concrete and diverse practices that are performed in the city, or even in direct opposition to them, undermines or even directly dismantles the 'right to the city', the right to practice diversity, to participate in the creation of shared urban places. This one of the major themes of Henri Lefebvre's critique (1996a) – a theme that is taken up in many of the contributions to this volume.

Encountering materiality

Encountering urban places is also encountering their concrete materiality. Encountering an urban place, one feels the materiality and atmosphere with all the senses and potentials of one's own body, with one's corporality (Merleau-Ponty 1962). The material arrangement of a place, the planning and building process, is the result of political decisions, of economic interests and of cultural dominations. The materiality of a place is the outcome of contests about the way it should be used; it is materialized and built power. Encountering the place, one feels and interacts with the power that is molded into the concrete materiality. In the place, the pavement guides the walker, the closed door stops the movement, and the uncomfortable bench discomforts the one who tries to rest. Materiality is more than the dead product of human labor and culture, following Latour (1993), it is an active participant (or 'actant') in social relations (see also Jackson 2000).

With respect to concrete materiality the particularity and diversity of urban places becomes apparent. Understanding the city as an *oeuvre* like Lefebvre does is helpful in putting the overwhelming diversity of urban places into perspective. The concept of *oeuvre* suggests that an urban place comes into existence through its diversity, a diversity that is encountered and savored by all senses.

If one considers the city as *oeuvre* of certain historical and social 'agents', the action and the result, the groups (or groups) and their 'product' can be clearly identified without separating them. There is no *oeuvre* without a regulated succession of acts and actions, of decisions and conducts, messages and codes. Nor can an *oeuvre* exist without things, without something to shape, without practico-material reality, without a site, without a 'nature', a countryside, an environment. (Lefebvre 1996b, 103)

Encountering urban places means always encountering a place with a specific history, specific representations, and a concrete materiality. How these places are reproduced is regulated by a state and by a city or other local or regional government, and their social structure is partly an outcome of a specific welfare regime. Urban places are always local entities, with their specific contestations and with their different, concrete encounters. In this book, the contributors do not simply encounter urban places, they are analyzing how encountering urban places evolves in places as diverse as Ankara, Cleveland, Frankfurt, Nowa Huta, London, São Paulo, New York, Kiel, and Vienna.

Encountering urban encounters

This book analyzes the encounters and the contestations they bring along in urban places: it offers analytic insights into contemporary cities, into places in which social order, identities, and exclusions are constantly brought into being, maintained, and transformed. The relationship of aesthetics, images, and material design to these spatialized processes and productions are the main object of scrutiny in this volume, and the readers of this volume themselves will encounter these relations in the following chapters, reliving urban encounters from distanced yet attached perspectives. What are the ties that bind these perspectives together?

One of these ties is the aesthetics of urban life – they are of a curious quality, one that is both highly visible and hidden, both openly effective and subtly influencing. Aesthetics are images and imaginations, and experiencing and performing material design. These active aesthetics participate in the contested production of places: inclusion and exclusion, attraction and repulsion are intimately related to the specific aesthetics of a place; to the way it is built, to its resisting materiality, to its image in people's minds, to advertising, to the way people look and act in the place.

The studies gathered in this volume will open windows and gates that allow analytical access to the processes of attraction and repulsion that evolve in urban spaces. The windows will provide a view on the visual aspects of urban life – answering questions about how people and things are perceived and how they present themselves, about which images are produced and reproduced, and about the construction of identities in urban spaces. The gates will allow access to realms beyond the visible, to voids and niches, rigid obstacles, bodily practices and to the seductions of urban life. Both gates and windows will let the reader encounter specific localities and people. The encounter – with people of different ethnicities, with friends, with a place's history, of photographer and photographed – is the interface to which the studies in this volume are linked. The detailed analysis of different kinds of encounters in different places offers a very close, rich, and accurate view on the city as a global phenomenon. Taken together, the articles that are presented in this publication produce more than a kaleidoscopic picture of this phenomenon;

they provide the reader with intimate insights to the both socially and aesthetically construed relations between places, images, and people.

One of the main themes that flows through the texts is the examination of the practices and performances of actors in the city. Practices of seeing are profiled in this volume; both as a part of the scientific enterprise itself – be it in the photographic occasion that is the basis of street photography or be it in the carefully arranged collection of people, buildings and artifacts in visual analysis – and as a part of everyday life in the city, where people are looking at things, watching others, or just letting their gaze pass over their surroundings. These practices of seeing are the counterparts of performances, or practices of displaying. Security personnel and prostitutes, artists and the unemployed inhabitants of deindustrialized cities, they all display their identities, contest the representations of others in public, catch an eye or make the gaze turn away. As has already been said, the embeddedness of these visible practices and performances into the city as a material place is another main theme that is carried through the volume. The interactions between the design of plazas, streets and buildings and the behavior of people in these places take place on many different levels, ranging from the obvious channeling and blocking of movements to subtle adaptations to light, sound, smell, and haptic impressions. The materiality of places is also actively deployed by actors. The skyline of metropolitan areas is both seen and lived in by the people who work there, but it is also reproduced in the stories they tell about their careers. At the same time, young adults might use the streets for their pleasure at night, contrasting the daily images of power and hierarchy with practices of evasion and spontaneity. Everyday life in the city is lived in contested places. In this book, the encounters in which contemporary urbanity is negotiated are unfolded using a shared perspective on the aesthetics of visual and material practices.

Investigating encounters

The reader will encounter the urban places in this book in chapters based on empirical or fieldwork. The chapters are based on data collected by walking along the streets and public spaces of different cities, by watching the people that use them, and by analyzing representations of places in the media or in exhibitions. The data was collected in the form of photographs, film and field notes, sketches, interview sequences, and observations. In all the different articles of this volume, images and perceptions play a crucial role. The transdisciplinary approach to urban aesthetics that has been chosen for this publication draws on the full spectrum of the visual (re)presentation: the artist-photographer's perspective, the systematic photography of the sociologist, photography as a tool for the analysis of social processes, the in-detail interpretation of video clips, and the use of maps and drawings both as ideals and analytic tools. The visual is in different ways directly bound to the text and is used to widen the exploration of urban places. This close connection is even further explored in the concluding chapter of this volume, which discusses the different ways imagery is employed in the different chapters.

Structuring encounters

The next chapter, written and photographed by Helen Liggett, builds on this introduction but brings it into the realm of real and concrete encounters. 'Urban Aesthetics and the Excess of Fact' uses photographs to tell a story about urban encounters and accompanies this story with an analysis of contemporary theories of space and presentation, exploring responses to the crisis of maintaining and fostering successful zones of contact in cities. Three examples for an 'excess of fact', that is, spatial practices beyond the realm of the institutionalized building of a city, are presented. Each is based on an aesthetics of existence in which the capacity to inhabit indeterminacy is combined with participation in the production of one's own circumstances.

In 'Perception, Aesthetics, and Envelopment – Encountering Space and Materiality' by Lars Frers, the phenomenological circumstances of participating in urban encounters in material buildings are examined. Analyzing video sequences, the experience of enveloping oneself, one's body, and one's activities is unfolded. The ways in which actors manage and deal with the ambivalences of everyday life in the city are scrutinized and the term 'envelopment' is presented as a tool that helps understand the movements between detachment and involvement with one's social and material surroundings.

In 'Eye-Catchers. Staging the Sociosexual – The Example of Prostitution', Martina Löw analyzes, ethnographically, the spaces of prostitution. They serve as the empirical base for a reconstruction of the gender-specific arrangements typical of sexwork. As with any social encounter, the cultures of visualization and aesthetic formation are the essential elements here that define the context of prostitution.

Accepting everyday urban practices and spaces as a potential source of information, Deniz Altay's chapter 'Urban Spaces Re-Defined in Daily Practices – "Minibar", Ankara' investigates a significant phenomenon called 'Minibar' – a space created by young people through appropriating the left-over spaces of the street by performing a specific leisure activity – and suggests that the city inhabitants are able to create spaces by re-defining the urban environment through their particular ways of using it. In addition, the author argues that the inhabitants have the possibility to resist and express issues concerning them through these spaces and practices.

'An Uncommon Common Space' by Zeuler R. Lima and Vera M. Pallamin presents the genealogy of Terraço do Trianon as a referential collective space in São Paulo, highlighting the relationship between physical and visual aspects and socio-political practices. Created as part of a park in the early 20th century, the terrace was reshaped in the architecture of the Museum of Art of São Paulo. This space represents how cultural institutions, public administrations, civil society, and the citizen have imagined, claimed, and occupied common open spaces in the city through uncommon social and cultural relations.

In 'Seeing Succession in Little and Big Italy – Encountering Ethnic Vernacular Landscapes', Jerry Krase's study of visual encounters in urban neighborhoods in the United States and Italy is demonstrating how the meanings of neighborhood spaces are changed by the agency of their inhabitants. Italian American neighborhoods in New York City are similar to Italian neighborhoods in Rome, in the way that they have been changed by the invasion of new and different ethnic groups. The spatial and semiotic logic of diasporic/transnational processes is presented here in the form of images; especially of changing commercial vernacular landscapes.

Lars Meier demonstrates in 'Working in the Skyline – Images and Everyday Action' how the 'global elite' encounters the city. Performing an ethnographic study of German bankers in their everyday life in the City of London and in Brixton, the power of the local, but also the power of specific inscriptions in the local is investigated in its translation to everyday life in the places frequented and evaded by the bankers. In focusing on these places the everyday actions of the so-called 'global elite' is bound to the place and the concrete, perceivable materiality of the place comes into focus.

In the paper 'Simulation or Hospitality – Beyond the Crisis of Representation in Nowa Huta' Łukasz Stanek examines the representations of space in Nowa Huta – an industrial city in Poland founded by the communist regime – and how these representations have been instrumentalized by commercial, political, and artistic practices in the last fifteen years. Based on writings by Henri Lefebvre, the paper investigates the practices of representing space as influencing investment, design, perception, use, and experience of urban space. Special attention is given to simulation as the widespread tendency of representing Nowa Huta and to ways of opposing it by introducing an alternative concept of representation of the city.

Katharine S. Willis shows in 'Sensing Place – Mobile and Wireless Technologies in Urban Space' that we live, act, and orient ourselves in a spatial world that is richly and profoundly differentiated into places. However, in a mobile society with ubiquitous access to – mostly invisible – communication technologies, perceptions of space are changed. In the increasingly mediated environment of urban public space this gives rise to a series of significant transformations. Instead of thinking of places with boundaries around, these spaces can be imagined as flows in networks of social encounters and situations.

In the final chapter, 'Working with the Visual', the editors analyze the diverse visual representations gathered in this book, bringing them together in a discussion of the different ways in which visual representations are used in this volume. They are looking at the benefits and potential drawbacks of the different ways in which photographs, maps, drawings, and videos are and could be used.

Following Lefebvre's notion from the beginning of this introduction that '(social) space is a (social) product', the textual and visual encounters with urban places in this volume provide vivid insights to the social and material production of the urban realm, to the struggles for representation and materialization in urban places.

References

Barnes, T. and Duncan, J. (eds) (1992), *Writing Worlds. Discourses, Text and Metaphor in the Representation of Landscape* (London: Routledge).

Duncan, J. and Ley, D. (eds) (1993), *Place/Culture/Representation* (London: Routledge).

Jackson, P. (2000), 'Rematerializing Social and Cultural Geography', in *Social and Cultural Geography* 1, 9–14.

King, A.D. (ed.) (1996), *Re-Presenting the City – Ethnicity, Capital, and Culture in the 21st Century Metropolis* (Houndsmill: Macmillan).

Kofman, E. and Lebas, E. (eds) (1996), *Henri Lefebvre – Writings on Cities* (London: Basil Blackwell).

Latour, B. (1993), *We Have Never Been Modern* (Harvard University Press).

Lefcbvre, H. (1991), *The Production of Space* (London: Basil Blackwell).

Lefebvre, H. (1996a), 'The Right to the City', in Kofman, E. and Lebas, E. (eds).

Lefebvre, H. (1996b), 'The Specificity of the City', in Kofman, E. and Lebas, E. (eds).

Merleau-Ponty, M. (1962), *Phenomenology of Perception* (London: Routledge & K. Paul Humanities Press).

Said, E. (1978), *Orientalism. Western Conceptions of the Orient* (Harmondsworth: Penguin).

Sennett, R. (1994), *Stone and Flesh – The Body and the City in Western Civilization* (New York: W.W. Norton).

Shields, R. (1996), 'A Guide to Urban Representation and What to Do About It – Alternative Traditions of Urban Theory', in King, A.D. (ed.).

Chapter 2

Urban Aesthetics and the Excess of Fact

Helen Liggett

Figure 2.1

The city, which is the name of assembled humanity [...] (Badiou 2005, 16)

Introduction

The aesthetics of urbanism, that is, how we seek to perfect assembled humanity, is both embedded in and removed from urban life. As the theorist Henri Lefebvre suggests, city plans exist as representations of space while at the same time urban space itself is constituted by the spatial practices of everyday life (Lefebvre 1991; 1996). It is in the encounters of daily life that the reach for experience presents itself.

Street photography is a procedure that connects daily life to representation and thus it is characterized by what photographer Lee Friedlander calls an 'excess of fact'. 'It's a generous medium, photography', he writes (Armstrong 2005, 293). In part this is a description of the type of photography he produces. But it is also an acknowledgement of how crowded the referent in un-staged photography necessarily is. Photographic space is more complex than a photographer's interest in a single object or viewers' tendency to think of images as being about a single subject. The complexity of any site generates a photographic space that leads to the proliferation of meaning in much the same way that urban life is not fixed, but constantly in motion. The visual cacophony produced by street photography evokes a radical urban aesthetics by pointing to the gap between the work and an audience's reading of it. What is radical about the excess of fact is that a space is both presented and unfinished. What is radical about contemporary urban life is just how crowded and unresolved it has become. Both suggest the need to explore the productive consciousness and creative imagination at the center of efforts to successfully constitute urban life and inhabit the city.

Figure 2.2

In idealizing the city, American urban designers have always had Europe. For example, there is the requisite year in Florence for serious architects and artists, and also the Amsterdam beloved of urbanists; each contributing to a widely recognized *doxa* about what vibrant city life could be like if only Americans would attend to their gutted inner cities, wean themselves from private transportation, reject the growth paradigm, overcome the inability to be impractical, and atone for other sins.

The intellectual context for these conventional aspirations is the classical liberal model of governance in which claims to legitimacy are based on the consent of the individual citizens. This scheme depends on principles of assembly in which the individual is logically prior to society. This includes taken for granted spatial configurations of modernity in which nation-states and national citizenship are the primary spatial units and markers of identity (Brenner *et al.* 2003). Quietly underpinning the belief in universal rationality in our own image is an aesthetics based on the belief that there *is* an order of things. Challenging this view, the realities and dangers of disassembly in cities throughout the world suggest that disruptions in urban spatial practices may not be addressed successfully from perspectives based in abstract universal humanism and the assumption of shared horizons. Globalization theory has focused on articulating transformations in the nation-state as the site of legitimate authority and policy formation, thus recognizing loosening of the tight logic connecting state, citizen, governance and identity (Brenner *et al.* 2003; Cheah and Robbins 1998). But there has been a tendency to bypass the city and its historical relationship to citizenship and civilization itself.

Yet, metaphorically speaking, if nations are how we plan, cities are where we live. If cities are examined as sites of human assembly, the deepest problems facing cities today are not about physical boundaries but the issue of how to make the assembly cohere. At the same time, cities persist, even given their problematic aspects, in the practices of millions of daily encounters that promote connection. These ongoing negotiations that constitute urban life are analogous to the 'excess of fact' in photographic space. This chapter presents images of three modes of 'excess of fact' in urban life: (1) echoes, (2) encounters, and (3) exchange. They are overlapping forms of successful human assembly, albeit on a small scale, that enact a radical urban aesthetics by producing unfinished zones of contact. Each points towards aesthetics of existence that is not about a reach that may exceed our grasp, but is lodged in the capacity to inhabit indeterminacy and to participate in the construction of one's own circumstances.

Figure 2.3

Echoes and space in which one has a place

Leon Battista Alberti's *Art of Building in Ten Books* is an example of an urban aesthetics that produces a unified city in which assembly at all levels is oriented towards enhancing the life of the city (1997, original publication 1450). It goes without saying in Alberti's work that the city is the site and hope of civilized life. In this view, building a good city is inseparable from making a good society. As a reflection of this unity Alberti combines cognitive, practical, and moral discourse. His text is scholarly, practical, and ethical. He includes all levels and stages of city building from review of ancient wisdom on how to site a city, to detailed consideration of infrastructure, and elucidation of every aspect of public and monumental buildings, including even the management and layout of the summer home. Every aspect of building is assessed in terms of its beauty, and also its performative force in bringing about a harmonious ideal.

Alberti's approach is to first repeat the wisdom of Greek and Roman builders and then assess whether their precepts should be followed and where and how they should be amended. As befits the art of compromise that makes the actual art of city living possible, he never dismisses beliefs that are not his own out of hand, but reassesses them based on practicality and his aesthetic ideals. His definition of practicality is one that is recognizable today. For example, how one ought to attend to the climate; when and whether a building should be restored are questions he raises and addresses in terms of the physical and social contingencies of each building situation. In this way his position at the beginning of the Renaissance is quite understandable. It is the early formation of what would become a modern worldview based in empirical truth.

Alberti's moral center is defined by harmony. This includes harmony of physical form and individual structures but also goes beyond these to include harmony and balance as a way of life. The measure of the city is the enhancement of the lives of its citizens. This is not an equalitarian or democratic vision but it is a humanist vision in the fullest sense of the term. The proper city is physically beautiful and is also understood as the personification of civilization. The image of the city presented in Alberti's work is one in which urban space is tied to the capacity to be human.

If there are echoes of the ancients in Alberti's urban aesthetics, there are echoes of Alberti in ours. But at the same time there are great differences. Today it is more common to discuss and evaluate city building within fragmented professional practices. For example, economic development discourse is eminently practical, historic preservation is concerned about the physical beauty of the city, and social welfare professions address the wellbeing of citizens who aren't otherwise covered. The distance from Alberti's unified approach is even greater when one considers that enhancing the lives of the citizens as a measure of the city is less likely to appear in official representations of urban space than the issue of economic viability.

Figure 2.4

Echoes of harmony as a measure of successful human assembly still exist in urban life, however. One can look, for one example among many, at the physical and social spaces constituted by African American churches. Part of the power of these churches is their capacity to secure the image of an interior harmony in opposition to a hostile external reality. One could say that the excess of fact in urban life is raw materials that are taken inside, where they are transformed to construct a community. Within the physical and social spaces of the church, islands of harmony are created: special places of meaning and depth that provide ballast in the face of external chaos and exclusion. The core of this urban aesthetics is not doctrine or ritual but experience. To belong is to directly experience and construct space in which one has a place.

The image of membership is not one of citizenship, but of homecoming. This is often expressed in homilies and activities organized to express and enact the theme of being home and also feeling at home. It is echoed and re-echoed in the comfortable spaces and welcoming experiences within the church that make a home, that insist that one can always come back home and be welcome and that tie coming home to acceptance. The call and response of voices are its oral form. The participation of individual members in a wide range of activities, from worship to education to social services helps to constitute the identity of believers, as good people, as God's people in harmony with the facts of their existence. The echoing frame of the church as the center of one's life and the source of one's identity reaches back to the beginning of Christianity; at the same time this – the image of Christian life – is expressed in a way that addresses current conditions. The echoing spaces of the physical and living church are places of continual restaging to fit the shifting situations of urban life. Thus one technique for creating space in which one has a place while existing in a realm that may be characterized as an excess of negative fact is to constitute and reconstitute spaces that echo and repeat a world that one knows and also wishes to be the case.

Figure 2.5

Encounter and the right to the city

The scope of Alberti's work is matched in modern theory by the theoretical and moral reach of Henri Lefebvre's *Production of Space* (1991). In his own characterization of his project Lefebvre argues that his work supplements Marx's axiomatic use of value with a broader conceptual scheme based on assembly. As is characteristic of modern thought, Lefebvre does not concentrate on physical building except to critique specific examples. His main work is developing the conceptual tools for an active theory of space that sees space as a process. Thus Lefebvre focuses on movement through gesture, on modes of assembling space, and on specifying rhythms and patterns that make space and the selves that inhabit it. If Alberti's approach is geometric, working out each issue in terms of a set of foundational principles, then Lefebvre's is symphonic. He introduces, and doubles and redoubles his themes in numerous applications to produce reflections on how social and physical space are joined. Lefebvre's spatial theory includes a history of spatial development in the West and an innovative approach to the study of spatial practices, both tied to the development of an active urban aesthetics.

In Lefebvre's image of the fragmentation of modern life, there is separation between three modes of making space. Representations of space, that is space as conceived, have come to dominant city building. In spite of this, spatial practices of everyday life continue as what I have been calling excess of fact. That is, they are often peripheral to discussions that imagine and plan space within professional discursive practices. What Lefebvre calls representational space, that is, space constructing what it is to be human in the most profound ways, has become very limited. The dominance of representations of space, the urban spatial order organized by the roving eye of capital, dominates city building. As an example of these imbalances within contemporary European cities, Lefebvre is particularly critical of the city as a tourist destination site, drained of life and organized into separate and separating realms for show and for life.

The aesthetic he promotes, 'the right to the city', is outside of the dominant modes of assembly and the abstract logic that organizes them (Lefebvre 1996). The right to the city is centered in the excess of fact that constitutes daily life. The claim for the right to the city is the claim that the city can be the active space of human experience by fully realizing the unique spatial instances that are possible only in the diversity and density of chance occurrences of urban life. Lefebvre calls these moments 'urban encounters'. They are situated, unplanned connections with which city dwellers assemble space that they co-occupy and that cannot exist outside of their encounter. In these moments the city dweller again becomes a citizen.

Lefebvre's hope for the city is that the abstract representations of space that control the making of space, that constitute the citizen as consumer, and that require only rapt attention to the political spectacle that surrounds citizens, can be superceded in instances of mutually constitutive encounter. The gestures that make the space of encounter also make the subjects capable of it and re-affirm the city as a place of life (Liggett 2003).

One sees images of urban encounters in everyday fleeting contact between strangers who momentarily occupy the same space. We are familiar with moments of shared humanity in times of crisis. These moments are deeply non-instrumental in the sociological sense but foundational in the ontological sense. They bring to the surface how clearly we depend on each other to reaffirm our humanity. Lefebvre sees this type of human exchange as the key to making cities work.

Figure 2.6

His way of conceptualizing the space of encounter is not centered on planning festive events or meeting places for encounter. He is oriented towards an awareness of the potential of everyday life. Lefebvre was critical of planned or staged provocative encounters as some Situationalists defined them. Nor would he have been supportive of festive and themed marketplaces promoted and built by some American developers in the 1990s. The encounter is infinitely repeatable, in the sense that certain conditions such as the functional density and diversity of urban life make it possible. But this is different from any abstract proposal or plan for encounters because 'the right to the city' must be rooted in a way of life that Lefebvre hopes will return the city to life beyond the spectacle.

The urban encounter is not based on consent; it is based on an instant of connection. This momentary but infinite quality can be illustrated by applying the notion of urban encounter to street photography. Making a photograph on the street can produce an instant in which the photographer, urban space and the camera are united. It does not occur every time one photographs, but it is a photographic possibility embedded in the unpredictability of the street. It is mutually constitutive in the sense that it is reaching beyond making a picture to making the space of humanity. Photographers' evocations of photography as 'love' or 'a way of living' are images of this kind of photographic space.

Pointing out this resemblance between the urban encounter and street photography helps to highlight some of the dynamics of the encounter. It is, by definition, fleeting and it is, by definition, dependant on shared horizons (while it can also construct them). That is, at its best the urban encounter is an example of a meeting with the 'other' that produces mutually constitutive hybrid identities. One testimony to the viability of the urban encounter is how often people relate stories that are images of individual encounters in talking about why they like a city or to explain why they have choose to live an urban lifestyle.

Figure 2.7

Exchange and the dialogic occasion

The urban encounter can falter if the realm of shared horizons is so limited there is not enough raw material to construct space for a mutually constitutive moments. The opportunity for encounter to create a momentary hybrid space is decreased if residents of the city never cross paths. Similarly, if they understand themselves only in terms of mutually exclusive identities, the chances for encounter are radically reduced. The right to the city outlines an urban aesthetic, but Lefebvre did not emphasize the dynamics that produce connections between how we see ourselves and how we read others.

Further analysis of the mechanics of encounter can suggest how the fleeting victory of the ordinary encounter can be informative about the extraordinary achievement of living together.

The language of encounter does emphasize connection amid diversity, but at the same time, at some level it requires a shared horizon. This could be called aesthetics of diversity and difference within a frame. The city in this era of globalization is often populated by citizens whose identity is maintained by a combination of approximate exclusion and distant encounters. That is, people may live physically near each other but maintain their closest personal relations in distant places. In addition, the image of the city produced by the society of the spectacle assumes homogeneity exists and misses the fundamental differences on the ground on which we would like to stand.

Figure 2.8

If one returns to the photographic experience, one can suggest that characterizing it in terms of the photographer, the camera, and urban space, as I did above, considers only part of the process. Making a successful photograph is an open-ended project that necessarily involves more voices, including those of viewers. Although it is comforting to assume that a good photograph is a readable photograph, the excess of fact makes this too simplistic. In fact there are certain parallels between the recent interest in urban photography that is staged and the image of the city as out of control.

Outdoor photography that is staged or altered with artificial light can be seen on one level as an attempt to control image space. Images of space that one directs are an acknowledgement that both the excess of fact and the audience can't be trusted. From this point of view the referent and the readers cannot be left on their own because it is not clear how the making and reading of the image will turn out. Staged photography has produced some complex and beautiful work, but it also seems to be producing a new genre. This genre is closer to painting because it de-emphasizes the special characteristic of the photographic medium – that is, a relationship to the world as it is found. In classic street photography the excess of fact challenges, while widening, the horizons of the artist and viewer in making image space. In staged photography the excess of fact can be seen as a liability in the same way that different perspectives can be seen as a liability in governance and the law.

Just as Lefebvre laments the dominance of abstract modes of assembly, what he calls representations of space, the Russian literary theorist, M.M. Bakhtin is critical of formalist approaches in linguistics in general and literature in particular (1981). In *Discourse in the Novel*, M.M. Bakhtin argues that unity in language does not exist except perhaps for 'the mythical Adam' and in the critical approaches of literary scholars (1981, 279). Instead language always carries within it past and present systems of meaning, combinations of genres and ideologies – just some of the numerous contextual factors in play. The heteroglossic components of language recall Friedlander's comment about photography: 'It's a generous medium.' Bakhtin says 'Language [...] is overpopulated – with the intentions of others.' (1981, 294) Further, meaning in language is constructed in relationship. In a way similar to the necessary labors of the viewers in producing meaning from the photographic image, Bakhtin sees the listener as active: necessary to the construction of what he refers to as actual meaning. Intention and definition, like judgment and finality, are not useful notions in Bakhtin's image of discourse. Language is not a project based on discovering the truth of the object. It is an activity that is oriented towards an answer that requires a listener. That listener's ears are also heteroglossic. The system of meaning of the listener can condition the discourse to an extent that the object becomes incidental, or only an occasion for the generative powers of dialogue. Bakhtin suggests that '[t]he word lives, as if were, on the boundary between its own context and another, alien context.' (1981, 284)

Figure 2.9

It is this boundary, or gap that provides insight into the mechanisms of successful urban encounters. Encounters are not a meaning of minds; they are the occasions for the construction of minds. In other words, one model of an urban encounter implies something like a Wenn diagram. Encounter is possible to the extent that spheres overlap. A dialogic model based on Bakhtin's work suggests that the overlap is the effect of encounter – and it may not be an overlap, but a new creation. Dialogue is discourse that finds zones of contact by producing them.

It is not difficult to make an argument for the city as heteroglossic space. One of the most ubiquitous features of cities touched by globalization is their heterogeneity. They are concentrated spatial examples of how any discursive site contains many languages. One can argue that at some level heteroglossia within spared space is both the definition of urban life and also its greatest achievement. Two factors creating the gap between the potential for the city and life of citizens within it are the recruitment and voluntary movement of populations across national borders and the separation of identity from national citizenship. Not only do many people not live in the land of their birth, they may not plan to, and/or the state of their birth may no longer exist as a state. In addition, for some migrants, citizenship in their new residence may not be possible or desirable. Add to this the fact that the clearly defined nation state system has never existed wholly in fact in an uncontested way, and one can see some sense to one of the early statements in this piece that we may plan at the national level, but cities are where we life (Brenner *et al*. 2003). As Bakhtin's analysis of meaning suggests, in practice cities cannot be sites of the law, or of governance, unless they flourish as places of exchange.

The most familiar site of exchange in the city is the market. The principle of assembly in the traditional marketplace is not the commodity form of exchange. The commodity form puts value in the object, and buyers and salespersons have very little to do with each other as people or with creating new meaning. In the tradition barter sense of exchange, however, the object is the occasion for working out value in the context of a relationship between buyer and seller. The barter exchange is in this sense a dialogic occasion. In commodity exchange in the common retail form, relationship in any transaction is considered beside the point, an excess of fact. But barter requires interlocutors with personalities who engage each other. It is a space of encounter that begins with difference and moves toward the creation of value, rather than producing the mutual recognition of pre-existing values. The excess of fact that comprises the dialogic occasion of bartering makes this creation of meaning and value possible. What makes the dialogic occasion itself possible is not the imposition of law, but the presence of desire, the desire to create a shared space for the purposes of a achieving a successful transaction.

Figure 2.10

From this viewpoint the mechanism for successful encounter becomes the willingness to engage the 'other' in order to secure the 'self'. Each of the images of encounter discussed in this paper is an existing mode of human assembly in urban space. In each, human assembly is forged from different combinations of engagement at the level of identity and commitment to that engagement. None offers a totalizing solution for the ills that beset contemporary urban life. But each example offers insight into how the shared space that constitutes urban life is produced. In each, the willingness to risk the loss of the illusion of an independent existence is joined to the desire to gain the right to the city.

Appendix – note on images

The ten images that accompany 'Urban Aesthetics and the Excess of Fact' present a short parallel photographic sequence to the text. In photographic sequences as developed by Walker Evans (*American Photographs* 1938) and Robert Frank (*The Americans* 1958), photographs are presented in carefully constructed series in which the force of the connections among the images produce further meaning than that found in the individual images. Arranged without text or captions the sequence is a visual performance; in the cases of Evans' and Frank's work, of themes integral to American culture. In my use of photographic sequence I continue to use images as a language, to use internal elements to cite each other, and to build meaning by juxtaposition. In addition, images relate to the text as well as produce a parallel performance.

The sequence in this chapter moves from geometry to gesture. This is analogous to the argument in the text from abstract representations of space to concrete practice. In many of the images what I call 'an excess of fact' in the text is key to understanding them. The images also play with triangles and the numbers two and three in showing encounters and connections.

The introductory image is an example of 'assembled humanity'. It shows some of the beauty of public life of Darmstadt, where the conference on which this book is based was held. It is divided in half twice, once by the light and once by the water. That introduces geometry and a sense of balance. It contains a number of human elements, including discovery of the photographer. An example of movement in the whole sequence from geometry to gesture is seen in the third and eighth images, both from the same site in Darmstadt. The eighth cites the third because of the site, but they are very different in tone. The third image is oblique and formal, organized as a triangle. The eighth image is active and engaged and uses the light in a playful way. The use of the triangle in the third image is carried over from the second image, where triangles and the number three help organize the excess of fact. This is an oblique image in that the relationships between the shapes, stripes on the flags and the chairs, and the three generations of people do not produce any explicit meaning. As a result the effect of the image is unclear.

On the other hand, the effect is very clear in the fourth image, where Pastor Preston reaches across with a connecting gesture to a member of his church, while just in front of them two women are admiring a new baby. Following on this the fifth image shows a welcoming gesture that characterizes the worship experience. Also it features the women of the choir whose engagement is central to the church.

The sixth image is a repeat of the second, except it is very different. The triangles have been transformed into the space of engagement and the generations clearly have something to say to each other. This gesture is in public space but it carries meaning from the fourth image with the gesture reaching in the same direction. The seventh image is a public event characterized by explicit encounter and exchange between performer and audience. The ninth image moves this encounter into exchange among people who are demographically very different, but share the desire for exchange. The light is a major component here, as in the eighth image. The arms are repetition of gestures in previous images. The final image faces back over the whole sequence. It is also a display of desire in the street that trumps the law of partitioned business like street space.

If making photographs is not about capturing an object, but about making a space, then making good photographs means that photographic space always contains some element to be discovered. In successful sequences the connections are to be discovered and enjoyed by viewers. In this regard I hope this overview is not too detailed.[1]

References

Alberti, L.B. (1997), *On the Art of Building in Ten Books* (Cambridge, Mass: The MIT Press).

Armstrong, C. (2005), 'Lee Friedlander, Museum of Modern Art, New York', *ArtForum* September, 293–4.

Badiou, A. (2005), *Handbook of Inaesthetics* (Stanford: Stanford University Press).

Bakhtin, M.M. (1981), Discourse in the Novel, in *The Dialogic Imagination* (Austin: The University of Texas Press).

Brenner, N., *et al.* (eds) (2003), *State/Space* (London: Basil Blackwell).

Cheah, P. and Robbins, B. (eds) (1998), *Cosmopolitics. Thinking and Feeling beyond the Nation* (Minneapolis: University of Minnesota Press).

Evans, W. (1938), *American Photographs* (New York: Museum of Modern Art).

Frank, R. (1958), *The Americans* (Paris: Robert Delpire 1959).

Kofman, E. and Lebas, E. (eds) (1996), *Henri Lefebvre – Writings on Cities* (London: Basil Blackwell).

Lefebvre, H. (1991), *The Production of Space* (London: Basil Blackwell).

Lefebvre, H. (1996), 'The Right to the City', in Kofman, E. and Lebas, E. (eds).

Liggett, H. (2003), *Urban Encounters* (Minneapolis: University of Minnesota Press).

---

1   I would like to thank Lars Frers and Lars Meier for their steady and intelligent guidance of this project.

Chapter 3

Perception, Aesthetics, and Envelopment – Encountering Space and Materiality

Lars Frers

In this chapter, I will get involved in the physicality of everyday life in railway and ferry terminals. The analysis presented here will wedge itself between people and what they encounter. Feeling for the pressures and pulls that are exerted in between people and their surroundings, an analysis that traces the relations between perception and social-spatial-material constellations will be developed, offering the term 'envelopment' as a tangible approach to understanding the ambivalences of everyday life in the city.

In this in-between space, many things are happening in a constant flow of actions and events: people, things, and other people align themselves to each other, they collide with each other, sometimes changing in this process. Seen from a distance, these constant interactions between things and people can very well be interpreted as relations between entities of a similar status – as opposed to hierarchical subject-object relations. This perspective offers many opportunities for research into the relations between space, materiality, and people, as is witnessed by the numerous publications which make productive use of concepts like Bruno Latour's *actants* (Latour 1993; Latour 2005) or Andrew Pickering's mangle of practice (Pickering 1995). In my Ph.D. thesis, I am also working with these concepts to get a better understanding of the way architecture and technology interacts with people in terminals. In this chapter, however, I will take a different perspective on these relations. I will look at the in-between spaces, but I chose to look at them from the perspective of the actors themselves. How do they experience their interactions with the place, the stuff, and with the people they encounter? How do they perceive their environment and how may these perceptions find their way into what people actually do in places like railway and ferry terminals?

Answering these questions requires both theoretical decisions and empirical 'data'. The theoretical decisions that I made will be flagged in the course of this text – one of the major routes that I steered away from has already been mentioned: actor-network theory and related concepts. What about the 'data'? I collected it during stays in terminals, both as the product of participant observation and as the product of video recordings done with a digital video camcorder. In addition, I spent and am still spending a lot of time in railway stations and ferry terminals traveling between places – some unsystematic observations have been made during these occasions, and some of the pictures and video sequences have been taken spontaneously when something interesting was going on and I happened to have my camera or camcorder with me.

The video recordings are of particular value for this chapter because they allow me to see and hear one occasion repeatedly, and, as a result, analyze those fleeting moments and tiny adjustments that are happening in the in-between spaces and moments. It is during those moments and in these spaces that a quite peculiar process can be located, it is this process, called for lack of a better term 'envelopment', or *Einhüllung* in German, that I will discuss in this chapter.

Unease and materiality

In this section, I will try to track the roots of the term 'envelopment', to allow for a critical appreciation of its possibilities and limitations. Ever since finishing my diploma thesis on the Potsdamer Platz area in Berlin (Frers 2001), I was looking for something that could grasp the unease that I feel in many urban places, some kind of name or term to grasp the feeling that grows when spending time in places like the Marlene-Dietrich-Platz in the Potsdamer Platz area, or in modern or refurbished railway stations. In my experience and in my analysis of the Potsdamer Platz it became quite clear that the perception of my surroundings, of the concrete ways in which they are designed, had a distinct impact on the ways in which I felt and acted.

The search for a word to describe this feeling – a feeling that is based on a process of perception – got more and more specific during the years that followed. Pondering the experience of spending time in places that leave me with a certain unease and talking to others about this experience, it became clear that this feeling is on the one hand a very personal experience, not felt by everyone at the same place in the same way, but on the other hand it is a feeling that is experienced in a wide range of different places and experienced by different kinds of people. Intertwined with these different ways of feeling was another aspect. In situations where I felt uneasy, someone else might feel safe and comfortable. This ambivalence between unease and comfort was difficult to trace but it is at the heart of one of the bundles of roots that merge into the term 'envelopment': the search for a term to describe experiences that differ from person to person but that, in their ambivalence, are shared by these individuals and that are, though different, quite specific to the places in which they are experienced.

The next bundle of roots is originating in theoretical considerations. Inspired by concepts such as Foucault's panopticism (Foucault 1995), Deleuze and Guattari's rhizome (Deleuze and Guattari 1987), and other postmodern or poststructuralist approaches to the understanding of power, I was looking for a non-hierarchical concept of power and social control. This concept should make the productivity of these non-hierarchical approaches tangible, it should allow an understanding of the role that everyone plays in the creation of social control – a kind of control that originates at many places, in many people, that may flow in one direction, disposing people to do certain things and evade other paths of action (similar to Foucault's dispositives), but that may also collapse suddenly, disappearing into historical rifts. Everyone's participation in the permanent re-creation of the world, both as an active supporter, an active 'resister', or a more or less passively involved part of the social and material production of space should be touched by this term.

Another strand that grew into the term 'envelopment' comes from the recognition that the body plays a central role in the relations of space, materiality, and people. As Sennett demonstrates vividly in *Stone and Flesh*, the body, its corporality, and its flesh is in intimate contact with the city. Architecture is experienced by the body, pain and joy are bodily sensations that are in many ways specific to time and place, to the historically changing ways cities are built and used. Sennett's master image for the modern world is the 'passive body'. This passive body is only remotely connected to its surroundings, and for Sennett this remoteness raises a central critique of modernity:

> Lurking in the civic problems of a multi-cultural city is the moral difficulty of arousing sympathy for those who are Other. And this can only occur, I believe, by understanding why bodily pain requires a place in which it can be acknowledged [...] Such pain has a trajectory in human experience. It disorients and makes incomplete the self, defeats the desire for coherence; the body accepting pain is ready to become a civic body, sensible to the pain of another person, pains present together on the street, at last endurable – even though, in a diverse world, each person cannot explain what he or she is feeling, who he or she is, to the other. But the body can follow this civic trajectory only if it acknowledges that there is no remedy for its sufferings in the contrivings of society [...]. (Sennett 1994, 376)

I will neither discuss Sennett's notion of the multi-cultural city nor the connotations to Christianity in this context, instead, I want to focus on the role of pain and the sensitivity to the pain of the other. The lack of this sensitivity is exactly what makes the comforts of modern life and the distancing or remoteness that goes along with these comforts problematic. I tried to embrace this master image of the passive body and use *passivity* as the metaphor that should represent a central problem of contemporary urban life. However, I was justly criticized for using this term,[1] since passivity is only one side of the process that is actually happening – there is always a moment of active choice involved, even if it passes almost instantaneously and usually goes unnoticed. Deciding not to do something also requires effort, and this tiny but crucial effort might get lost if passivity is the lens through which one looks at urban life.

1   My thanks for this go foremost to my advisor Helmuth Berking, whose keen observations and comments are very helpful, enriching my empirical and theoretical efforts.

These are the general sources or roots that grew into the concept of envelopment, growing and developing in my mind when I spent time in terminals, thinking, looking for a word that would evoke the meaning of what I felt and what was part of my unease.[2]

Aesthetics and perception

Before spelling out what exactly is meant by the term envelopment, it should be made clear how perception – one of the basic moments of envelopment – is understood in this context and what role is played by the other element of this chapter's title: aesthetics. Aesthetics and aesthetical judgments are not understood as being striving for an ideal aesthetics, for beauty per se, or for a specific aesthetic quality such as Kant's sublime (Kant 1952). Instead, the aesthetics of our mundane, everyday surroundings are of relevance here. How do objects appear to us, how do we like their looks, their texture, their smell, sound, and mass? Design as a feature not only of particularly artistic products, but as a feature of all the things we use and interact with is of much greater significance for this work. Some things attract certain people; others are repelled by the same things. The smells of a bakery in the terminal may make your mouth water; the stench of the toilets may make you look for some other place to stay. The sunlight that is entering through the terminal's windowed ceiling may invite people to stand in its rays; shadows may make certain corners better be evaded in the late evening. The gentle curve of a bench and its wooden panels appear comfortable, while the iron grille and edgy corners of a metal seat may be perceived as cold and uninviting. These material aesthetics are the subjects of Böhme's phenomenological approach to a philosophy of design and materiality (see Böhme 1995).

Phenomenology is probably the most central tool for this analysis or, put differently, it is the lens through which the unfolding of human agency is observed here. Böhme in his 'new aesthetics' focuses on the role of nature in our life and the possible implications of a phenomenology that takes our relation to nature and the ecological movement into account. For this article, perception and processes of perception are crucial, therefore I will take a different turn in phenomenology than Böhme does – a turn that is going into the direction that Merleau-Ponty takes us in his *Phenomenology of Perception* (1962). Perception for Merleau-Ponty is not an analytical process that sets independent entities into relation with each other, be they things for themselves or be they the sensory data that is processed by individual sensual organs like the skin, the nose, the eyes, or the ears. Instead, perception is conceived as a 'live' process. Merleau-Ponty describes perception as it is experienced by the perceiving human being, as a process that

---

2   There are two other sources that probably made the concept of envelopment salient to me. One of them is Simmel's *The Metropolis and Mental Life* (1950), where he develops the notion of the 'blasé' attitude. The other, part of North American popular psychology, is the so-called 'personal bubble', a space that is closely attached to a person and more or less clearly delineated; if the border of this space is crossed, an intrusion of privacy is experienced and personal offence can be taken. Both of those sources have also been pointed out by the participants of the panel on which this volume is based.

always takes place in a specific context, as a process in which the relation of sensual impressions to expectations is quite intimate. These expectations, sometimes described as the horizons of perception and agency, are not just mental expectations based on evaluations of the current situation – they are produced by body and mind as one. The body for Merleau-Ponty is not restricted to the physical shell. In its corporality it encompasses perception, thought, and physical action; and, in his later work (Merleau-Ponty and Lefort 1968), corporality extends as the flesh, or *chair* in French, from the body to its surroundings. This is the perspective that is taken here: perception is a permanent achievement in which the corporality of the perceiving being is put into an intimate and encompassing relation with its sensual environment. All senses work together, they are directed to certain horizons, which in turn can shift and change in interaction with current circumstances.

This understanding of human experience is very closely related to the way in which ethnomethodology treats human agency.[3] The emphasis on process and context is shared by both. Agency or behavior in ethnomethodology is mainly seen as an unfolding sequence of acts in which actors take different turns, aligning themselves to preceding acts and constituting in each one of their acts the social and shared world on which we rely as the more or less normal environment of our everyday life. The constituents of a sequence of actions can be tiny: in conversation analysis it has been demonstrated that pauses with a duration of significantly less than one second are treated as being meaningful by the participants of a conversation. This zooming in or blowing up of sequences of acts reveals the permanently ongoing, fine-grained adaptation and mutual attention that people display to their environment, thus demonstrating social order as a process that is accomplished in real time by participants in a shared environment.

This ethnomethodologically informed attention to detail, to the fine-grainedness of human agency is the way in which I can delve into the in-between spaces and situations that happen when people align themselves with their material and spatial surroundings. Looking at the way someone will turn her or his head and shoulders for a brief moment while passing through a door, looking at short stops and phases of re-orientation, at irritations that happen when following a course of action, all of this reveals the subtle ways in which we align ourselves to our environment; at the same time, we shape our environment – depending on what we do we alter the circumstances, we make certain actions more salient to co-present others, we challenge the social order. This constant production, re-production, and challenging of social, spatial, and material order will be examined with the analytical tool that is being developed in this chapter: the term *envelopment*. Taking the perspective of the actors themselves, following the permanent and live unfolding of actions and events, inspecting subtle but powerful details, the term envelopment should make it possible to follow or re-feel (*nachfühlen* in German)

---

3 The close relation of ethnomethodology to phenomenology – particularly as championed by Alfred Schütz (1967) – is present in many of ethnomethodology's production (see Maynard and Clayman 1991).

how social-spatial-material constellations we enter in concrete places work, and how these constellations order our everyday lives.

Building the envelope

For the following part of this chapter, I chose one concrete situation – leaving a train at Kiel Hauptbahnhof (Kiel's main railway station, a stub terminal) – as an instance which is helpful for understanding the characteristics of envelopment as will be shown in the following. Since printed text is a linear medium, I will have to proceed in an analytical way. First, I will present the details that make up the setting which people enter when leaving this train: the material, spatial and social organization of the platform. Doing this, I will stage an interplay between text and pictures – to escape some of the linearity of a narration, to show some of the richness and complexity of the setting, and to give you as much raw stuff as I can in this context.[4]

Figure 3.1 Leaving the train
Source: Author

---

4   However, I do recommend visiting the website that accompanies this chapter (either search for the terms 'frers' and 'envelopment', or enter the URL http://userpage.fu-berlin.de/ ~frers/perception-envelopment.html). On this website, you can watch or download the actual video sequence from which the pictures have been taken. Watching the video repeatedly, focusing on different details, scrubbing through the video, and watching select passages frame by frame helps a lot in understanding what is going on and makes it possible to check the basis of my argument.

Figure 3.2 Entering the platform
Source: Author.

All of the pictures are still frames taken from a video sequence that I recorded on 1 September 2005. Below the pictures, you can see a time code and a marker. The first four digits of the time code give the current position in minutes and seconds, the last two digits give the number of the frame.[5] The marker shows the current position relative to the rest of the recording. Looking at the time code and the marker helps you to reconstruct the speed in which the events unfold and in which both I, wielding the digital camcorder, and others act and orient themselves in the spatial, material, and social organization of the platform.

Leaving the train, Figure 3.1 shows the presence of others passing by in the sunlight outside on the platform. On the platform, in Figure 3.2, captured 2.8 seconds later, I turn left after leaving the train, following others, who carry bags and pull trolleys. They pass by to the left of two obstacles, one a flower pot, the other a sand storage chest. It is between these moving people and the static, solid obstacles that I have to find my way, following others who want to get to the exit of the platform.

---

5   Since the video has been recorded in PAL format, one second consists of 25 frames.

Figure 3.3 Obstacles
Source: Author.

The obstacles displayed on Figure 3.3 make it even more evident how much management is involved in walking down the platform. Not only is it necessary to navigate one's own body through the moving people, in case of the woman on the picture it is also necessary to pay attention to the child that accompanies her – all of this while holding a sweater and keeping the trolley case under control. The slowdown that is caused by the simultaneity of these actions contrasts with the straightforward movement of the man who is at the same height with the woman on Figure 3.3, and seven seconds later is several strides further down the platform (see Figure 3.4). Additionally, the information that is given on the displays (Figure 3.3) might capture some attention – even though it could be hard to read against the bright sky reflecting on the glass of the display. On Figures 3.1 to 3.4 it also becomes apparent that the light is changing while walking down the platform. It begins with very bright sunshine that fades in a twilight zone into until we enter the shadowed and electrically lit passage along the platform.

On Figure 3.4 a few of the more immediate dangers that have to be taken into account while moving down the platform are visible: the train itself might start moving; its doors may open or close. There is a gap between the platform and the rails, opening to a space of lethal danger: the rails and the wheels of the train – the deadliness of this particular combination has been pondered by most users

Figure 3.4 Dangers

Source: Author.

of subway systems or railway lines. Most people will keep a significant distance between themselves and this gap.

Up to this point, I have only written about the visual and the bodily-material aspects of the setting. In the video clips, another sensual layer is added to the experience: sound. Walking down the platform, many different sounds are recorded by the camcorder; the most prominent being announcements made through the terminal's public address system and, more and more with each step that brings us down the platform, construction noise consisting of the screeching and hammering of metal working its way through other hard matter. This construction noise drowns almost all other sounds when it is at its peak.

Taken together, and not even paying particular attention to other aspects of the setting like temperature, wind, moisture, and smell, it becomes apparent that a multitude of perceptions is or can be made while the walking, rushing, standing, generally navigating through the setting is accomplished by the co-present actors in this setting. This is still not the whole experience of walking down the platform. Other thoughts cross the minds of those walking down, and one is not only attentive to the things present in the current field of sight, one is also aware of presences and actions that happen out of sight, behind your back, above the roof, or at the other side of the train.

Being enveloped

Leaving the train leads to an encounter with a specific social-spatial-material constellation. As has been described in preceding section of this chapter, this constellation is highly complex and consists of myriad impressions, all of which surround those who enter the setting almost immediately – enveloping them. This process of being enveloped by one's surroundings has many different aspects, which affect the quality of the envelope and the process of envelopment in ways that are specific to the setting that is encountered. Following is a brief list of the characteristics of the envelope:

- One of the most apparent characteristics of the envelope is the way it dampens or filters perceptions. Not everything is let through: a reduction in quantity and a qualitative shift occurs in the perception of the surroundings.
- At the same time, the envelope reduces the zone of bodily reach or activity. The envelope may be closer to the physical body of the person, limiting actions and gestures to ones that are oriented to oneself, or it may stretch out further, encompassing even people and things around the person.
- The envelope can also be thicker or wider in some places than in others. It may allow perceptions concerning a wide field in front of the person but limit the perception of what is going on above or behind or on one particular side of the person.
- The border of the envelope is not a thin, clearly delimited line: it should be imagined more like a zone of different composition and thickness, ranging from quite solid and thin to wooly and wide.

As may be gathered from the last point, the term envelopment does not refer to an 'object in the real world' or a measurable process. 'Envelopment' as a process or 'the envelope' as an entity are intended as images or imaginations in the sense created by Bachelard in his *Poetics of Space* (Bachelard 2003) – these terms should be seen as walking the difficult line between playfulness and solidity, between analysis and empathy – a tool to help understanding a corporeal feeling that is difficult to name.

The character of the envelope directs attention and activities to certain areas. Since it fades out certain impressions and lets others pass, the enveloped person is focusing on certain aspects of her or his surroundings, while others escape attention. In this regard it is quite similar to the *blasé* attitude as described by Simmel (1950) – it keeps out some impressions, making the rest easier to manage – and thus has a certain functionalistic turn to it. The function that the envelope serves is the protection of the individual from distraction and sensual risk, helping the individual to focus on certain areas. In everyday life this means that the envelopment that happens when someone enters a socio-material-spatial constellation makes people not look at others, not notice certain things around them, ignoring noises and the talk of others, reducing one's sense of smell, and evading physical contact with the surroundings. Seen from the outside, a shell or capsule[6] is being put around the people that encounter a setting like the railway platform.

Enveloping oneself

One of the problems that I had with the concept of passivity was that it made it appear as if people just let things happen to them (or to others around them), having no part in the events themselves. Accordingly, envelopment would not be a better concept if it too would only allow for reception, not for a co-production or participation in the process. This active aspect of the process of envelopment will now be put into focus.

Figure 3.5 Time and orientation
Source: Author.

---

6   For a long time, I was not sure whether to translate the German *Einhüllung* as 'encapsulation' or 'envelopment'. 'Encapsulation' has the interesting connotations of white bloods cells encapsulating foreign matter in the blood or of other organic tissue growing around foreign matter in plants. The capsule is stronger than the envelope, something that grows with time. 'Envelopment' has the benefit of being softer, quicker, and lighter, evoking a sense of the wrapping-around of sensual impressions is easier achieved. In addition, the term 'envelopment' has an interesting meaning in mathematics (and, applied, in acoustics), describing curves surrounding and delimiting the amplitude of other curves or mathematical functions.

Figure 3.6 Arranging stuff
Source: Author.

People who enter a setting envelop themselves too – the expression 'to brace myself for something' refers to a similar experience or act. Other tangible examples are the pulling together of a cloak, wearing of sunglasses, and listening to music through headphones. Generally, a central aspect of enveloping oneself is the directing of one's attention. By focusing on a specific task like leaving the train station, changing trains, or looking out for others waiting on the platform, supposedly non-relevant perceptions are not allowed to pass through. This 'active filtering' is more complex than it may sound.

Changing trains may require simultaneous attention to time, the way from one platform to another, possible announcements regarding changes in schedule and platform, and so forth. Meeting others may require a very different stance if one is looking for a lover than if one is looking for a business partner or even a stranger one has never met before. Bodily posture, facial expression, and the way one feels may vary on a wide spectrum. Nonetheless, people's attention will be directed to specific things, and the envelope will be shaped accordingly. The look to the clock on Figure 3.5 and the arranging of one's stuff (Figure 3.6) are hints at what may occupy the attention and thus shape the envelope.

The shape, texture, and especially the circumference of the envelope will generally be influenced by the mood one is in. Being in a hurry shapes the envelope in a way that shuts out as many things as possible that (again, supposedly) have nothing to do with the reaching of the goal, opening it to certain perceptions in front and keeping it dense in all other areas. Being frightened, one produces a very tight envelope, which may even feel like a clasp. However, other moods can also open up the envelope; taking one's time allows for perceptions that are usually not made, giving attention to details or aspects that would not be let through normally. An interesting case would be absent-mindedness – some vague, general attention is being paid to the surroundings, but there might also be sudden openings in the envelope.

In this chapter, I do not have the space to provide empirical furnishings for these personal aspects of the envelope using the video recordings that I have made. I am not yet sure, in how far this will be possible, although I am confident that at least some hints of the directedness of the envelope and of the enveloping effects of mood can be gleaned from paying very close attention to the video. For this more immediate context, I will have to rely on the productivity of the image evoked by the term and by the examples that I wrote down above.

Figure 3.7 Down the platform
Source: Author.

Figure 3.8 End of platform
Source: Author.

Passage through envelopes

The last characteristic of the envelope that I will sketch out in this chapter is that it can consist of multiple layers – layers that are acquired and that will fall off, be shrugged off, or just slowly erode. How this moving through different kinds of envelopes can take place will again be demonstrated using stills from the video that I captured after leaving the train in Kiel.

One particularly remarkable aspect of the setting is the construction noise that has already been mentioned. Stepping out of the wagon, this noise is very much present, only to get even louder when one walks down the platform. Since the construction happens in the area at the end of the station's hall, where it opens up to the outside, the further one goes down the platform and into the hall, the less one hears the construction noise. As I argued above, for protection from the high-volume screeching and hammering an envelope is generated, perceptions related to hearing are being reduced, a general awareness of potential hazards coming from above, and a tightening of the envelope are some of the features of an envelope that would be produced in interaction with the noise. When one walks away from the noise, it becomes less audible with every step. The process that accompanies this growth of distance could be characterized as a slow erosion of the envelope – it becomes thinner and wider until it fades away completely. At the same time, other things happen and other perceptions are made, producing their own envelopes.

Figure 3.9 Turning head
Source: Author.

Figure 3.10 Exit
Source: Author.

The change of light and the widening of accessible space are also changing the envelope's layers. This dynamic process can be perceived if one sees Figures 3.7 to 3.9 as a sequence: walking down the platform to its end (Figures 3.7 and 3.8) and entering the reception hall, new perception-activities are available, grasping these, some people's heads are turning from left to right (Figure 3.9), the pace might be reduced or increased, looking up becomes more appealing because of the texture of the freshly renovated wooden ceiling, and because of the main display of departures that is hanging at the wall above the main entrance. At the same time it has to be decided if the seductions of the stores surrounding the main hall are being ignored or inspected. Depending on the outcome of these decisions, depending on the intensity of the

Figure 3.11 Outside
Source: Author.

bakery's smells, of the person's current mood, and on the presence and behavior of co-present others, another layer might be produced that shuts out all of these attractions, reducing the options, and leading the way to an exit or another platform.

The final sequence of video stills (Figures 3.10 to 3.12) demonstrates a remarkable change in the process of envelopment. The very bright light[7] outside the

---

7   The video recording shows a much stronger contrast than most people would experience with their own vision—the perceived contrast would depend on the age and the sensitivity to light, but also on the current emotional state of the person that is approaching the exit.

Figure 3.12 View
Source: Author.

exit on Figure 3.10 prepares for what is to come: a sudden change. However, more than the amount of light changes when one leaves the eastern exit of Kiel's Hauptbahnhof. A completely new scenery or field of perception becomes available.

This profound change from a closed, interior space with artificial lighting, reduced extension to the sides, and relatively clear options for action (standing and waiting, shopping, consuming, or passing through), to an open space with a wide horizon – in the direction of the harbor limited only by the curve of the globe – with many different things and people, a stairway that leads down into the scenery, wind that is blowing, and a change in temperature and humidity – perceiving and being part of this field causes several layers of the envelope to either change or fall off completely in a matter of seconds.

This sudden change, this shedding of layers and widening of the remaining envelope is accompanied by and displayed through behaviors that I could frequently observe at this location: people stop or pause (*innehalten* would be a proper term for this in German). They became part of a significantly different spatial-material-social constellation, requiring a reorientation on their part – a look at the time code below Figures 3.11 and 3.12 shows how long this took for the man wielding the bicycle: more than 20 seconds. On the video recording, I myself stop right after passing through the exit too. I let the camera scan over the surrounding area and zoom it in on the ferry, which will depart with me for Oslo a few hours later.

In itself, such a change in scenery does not necessarily cause a stop. To reiterate the point: the condition for this pausing is a change in perception, not a change in environmental factors or the sensitivity of a physical organ. If one is familiar with the setting, knows about view and weather, is in a real hurry, or otherwise preoccupied, the things one perceives might well not change so drastically, the perception focusing instead on potential hazards like wind, other people, and the stairs that have to be descended. My pausing in the video can, to some degree, be attributed to the lack of pressure that I felt at the time of recording – even though I knew the setting, knew that the harbor was outside of this exit and that the ferry would be moored to its berth, the sunlight and the attractiveness of the scenery enticed me so much that I changed my intention of producing a straight recording of the passage from the railway station to the ferry terminal – opening a gap for enjoying the view and breathing some of the coastal atmosphere.

Envelopment and encounters – risk and safety

The images, the descriptions, and the small stories that I have presented in this chapter serve to show that envelopment is both a tangible and concrete, and an imagined and fleeting process. Some of the bollards to which the concept of envelopment has been tied are the concrete material, spatial, and social features of the actor's environment. The design of places, their aesthetics – relating to all of the senses – and the potential field of activities that they offer, enters an intimate relation with the people who are present in this place, who are using it and thus participate in its production. Other ties are less tangible, relating to the moods and feelings of the people that are enveloped and that envelop themselves. These ties I have tried to show too, by telling about my own feelings and reactions, and by paying close attention to the subtle adjustments displayed by others whom I have recorded, making their activities available for detailed and repeated scrutiny. Both solid and fleeting aspects of the process of envelopment have been inspected and, taken together, they produce envelopes of specific characters, relating to the design of the places which people encounter in their everyday lives. Understanding the envelope as something that is co-produced by actors and their surroundings evades the traps inherent to concepts of passivity, enabling the analyst to untangle the different strands that are woven into the envelope. Following, I will again list some of the potential features of envelopes – again, the list is neither exclusive nor complete. It is intended foremost as an impulse for the imagination and, to some degree, as a guide to reflection on the ways one feels when walking through everyday life, encountering people and places, acting in certain ways, not following other paths of action.

The envelopes that are produced in social-material-spatial constellations have a certain thickness, filtering or dampening perceptions more or less strongly. The envelopes also have different circumferences: they can be very wide, opening spaces for interaction; or they can sit close and tight, keeping one's attention focused on the care for one's own corporality. The envelope is not necessarily smooth and uniformly spherical. It can bulge out at certain points, be tighter in some areas that in others, be of a different texture in front than above, and so forth. The envelope does also not necessarily consist of a single sheet. It can be made up of several stacked layers, sheets which can fall off without affecting other layers that are related to different perceptions.[8] Taken together, the process of envelopment produces a dynamic and complex layering that affects the way in which people relate to their environment. Since perceiving as it is understood by Merleau-Ponty cannot be separated from acting, the effects that the process of envelopment has on perception is also an effect on the multiple ways in which we interact with our environment. The process of envelopment is intended as one way to approach what Lefebvre has analyzed as *The Production of Space* (1991).

This is not to say that envelopment is a clearly definable and unproblematic concept. Who envelops whom? Is it the place or the social-spatial-material setting enveloping the person? Is the person mainly enveloping him- or herself? It is difficult if not impossible to decide these questions and, for example, to locate concrete processes on a continuum from active to passive. It is also difficult to trace the feelings and moods of those who are participants of the constellations that we encounter. It is even difficult to keep track of our own feelings, spontaneous reactions, and of all the things we do – usually without being particularly aware of them at any given moment.

Nonetheless, the concept of envelopment has a lot to offer for helping to understand the ways in which our lives unfold at concrete places. In this chapter, I have developed envelopment as a concept, I have not yet applied it as an analytical tool. However, in this conclusion, I will try to sketch some of the perspectives it offers, perspectives from which one may be able to formulate a critique of urban places, of concrete material-spatial-social constellations. A particular benefit of the concept of envelopment is the ambivalence that it harbors. This ambivalence makes it obvious that there is no perfect design, that the unification of places according to one particular ideal is problematic and that conflicting uses and practices should be taken into account. What is this ambivalence? On the one hand, the process of envelopment reduces the risks of everyday life. It shuts out many irritations. The envelope protects its bearer from potentially harmful involvements. It heightens comfort, is something one could huddle into, sheltering from outside influences. It may also provide an increase in efficiency, focusing one's attention on the tasks at hand. On the other hand, however, the process of envelopment reduces one's engagement in and towards one's environment. A tight envelope will not let seductions pass. The chances of an encounter with a charming stranger, the possibility of taking pleasure in the aesthetics of some thing or event, the number of handles by which one can change and affect one's environment – all of these opportunities pass by much more easily. Coming back to the citation from *Stone and Flesh* that I gave in the section on 'Unease and Materiality', the chances for

---

8   It might also be interesting to think of the envelope as having folds in some places. What could these folds conceal? Where and why would they be lifted?

paying attention to the experiences and the corporeal sufferings of others are greatly diminished by a set of strong and tight envelopes. Sympathetic involvement in one's surroundings is not easily achieved if one does not perceive the many sufferings and the many opportunities for joy or pleasure that are potentially available in one's surroundings. Following these ambivalences is, I think, taking me along the path that to an understanding of the unease that I am feeling in many places. Places like a modernized railway station offer many interesting possibilities: there are many other people, there are shops, there is a mixture of architecture, art, and advertising that may be more or less interesting or pleasant. However, certain features of these places – the way advertisements are placed, the non-availability or secure design of waiting facilities, the presence of security personnel, the focus on consumption, the way visibility is produced (Frers 2006) – work together to produce an envelope that makes managing my affairs an easy and smooth experience, but also an experience that lacks involvement, that lacks sympathy and room for encounters that may enrich the lives of their participants.

In this way, the ambivalences of the concept equal the ambivalences of everyday life in the city. Walking the line between comfort and excitement, between efficiency and leisure, between protection and risk is an everyday affair. This chapter argues that this everyday affair is based on perceptions of the aesthetics of the city and its places. In interaction with these aesthetics, with the design of places and with their uses, envelopes are generated which regulate our perceptions, thus regulating our involvement in our surroundings. The concept of envelopment is both inherently ambivalent and intended as an image or imagination, not a technical term accurately describing a measurable process. It should evoke a sense of what we experience and help understand why we do certain things, why we are complying with specific orders that are established in space, matter, and social rules – and when and why we might find opportunities for challenging these orders.

References

Bachelard, G. (2003), *Poetik des Raumes* (Frankfurt am Main: Fischer).

Berking, H. *et al.* (eds) (2006), *Negotiating Urban Conflicts – Interaction, Space and Control* (Bielefeld: Transcript Verlag).

Böhme, G. (1995), *Atmosphäre – Essays zur Neuen Ästhetik* (Frankfurt am Main: Suhrkamp).

Deleuze, G. and Guattari, F. (1987), *A Thousand Plateaus* (Minneapolis: University of Minnesota Press).

Foucault, M. (1995), *Discipline and Punish – The Birth of the Prison* (New York: Vintage Books).

Frers, L. (2001), *Den Marlene-Dietrich-Platz Erleben – Konstellationen im Stadtraum* Diplomarbeit. (Freie Universität Berlin).

Frers, L. (2006), 'Pacification by Design – An Ethnography of Normalization

Techniques', in H. Berking *et al.* (eds).

Kant, I. (1952), *The Critique of Judgement* (Oxford: Clarendon Press).

Latour, B. (1993), *We Have Never Been Modern* (Cambridge, Mass: Harvard University Press).

Latour, B. (2005), *Reassembling the Social – An Introduction to Actor-Network-Theory* (Oxford: Oxford University Press).

Lefèbvre, H. (1991), *The Production of Space* (Oxford: Blackwell).

Maynard, D. and Clayman, S.E. (1991), 'The Diversity of Ethnomethodology', *Annual Review of Sociology* 17, 385–418.

Merleau-Ponty, M. (1962), *Phenomenology of Perception* (London: Routledge & K. Paul Humanities Press).

Merleau-Ponty, M. and Lefort, C. (1968), *The Visible and the Invisible – Followed by Working Notes* (Evanston, Ill: Northwestern University Press).

Pickering, A. (1995), *The Mangle of Practice – Time, Agency & Science* (Chicago: University of Chicago Press).

Schütz, A. (1967), *The Phenomenology of the Social World* (Evanston, Ill: Northwestern University Press).

Sennett, R. (1994), *Stone and Flesh – The Body and the City in Western Civilization* (New York: W.W. Norton).

Simmel, G. (1950), 'The Metropolis and Mental Life', in K.H. Wolff (ed.).

Wolff, K.H. (ed.) (1950), *The Sociology of Georg Simmel* (Glencoe, Ill: Free Press).

Chapter 4

Eye-Catchers.
Staging the Sociosexual –
The Example of Prostitution

Martina Löw

In its spring catalogue, Faller, a well-known German manufacturer of model railroads and accessories, presents its newest products in the sector. This year these novelties include an assembly kit called the 'Lavender Owl Nightclub'. According to the catalogue, the kit includes 'a blinking red light and five persons plying their trade'. On the one hand, we may conclude without further ado that this innovation in the toy market is closely bound up with a liberalization of attitudes toward sexwork. Even children can now set up their own little prostitutes along their railroad line and steer their trains into a highly specific fairytale world. Still, and on the other hand, this development is nothing all that new, either. Fathers and their sons continue to constitute the majority of those devoted to small-gauge railroads, living out their male dreams in dark, secluded hobby cellars. It is thus only logical that their socialization in the red-light milieu should start out not only with stream engines and track sizes but also with Lavender Owls and those plying their trade in them.

In what follows I will analyze ethnographically the spaces and places of prostitution. These will serve as the empirical base for a reconstruction of the gender-specific arrangements and encounters typical of sexwork and the important role of aesthetics to create the special red-light atmosphere. The present paper centers on the findings of three months of research conducted at the International Research Center for Cultural Studies (IFK) in Vienna. The paper is furthermore based on a research project (DFG) on 'The Effective Structure of Space and Gender: the Example of Prostitution in Frankfurt am Main'. Apart from evaluations of observations and documents, both projects are based on expert interviews with prostitutes, social workers and police officers, affected neighbors, and legal practitioners.

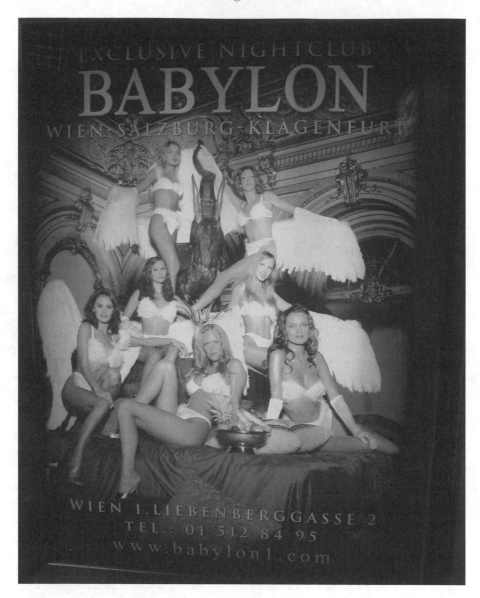

Figure 4.1 Poster Babylon
Source: Author.

On the ground: arriving in Vienna

I fly into Vienna. Posters announce to the new arrival what the town has in store for her. The first picture: Welcome in Schönbrunn. Vienna is known for its emperors and kings, famed for its empresses Sissi and Maria Theresia. It was the latter who had prostitution banned throughout Austria. The poster likewise makes reference to the zoo as an idyllic setting for children and as a trove of images of nature. The second poster is devoted to art. Vienna successfully markets itself as a stronghold of the arts. Now it must be music's turn, I think. 'Wine, woman, and song', as the guidebook puts it. But 'woman' comes only after Schönbrunn and Giorgione.

When you leave the arrivals section, you can't miss the Babylon's attempts to woo customers, old and new. Babylon, symbolic of mankind's attempt to approach God, and its failure, stands for the birth of diversity no less than for the lack of ability to understand it. Women on the poster welcome me, all of them white-skinned, and all of them clad in innocently white undergarments. Angels, creatures without gender and sexuality! And yet – the lascivious posture of the ladies seated on red satin seem suggestive of something. But of what? I think of a musical theater, of a movie poster. Who would have thought that Vienna's noble brothel would advertise here at the airport? Only those in the know. The poster must be meant as a welcome to the regular customer. And be geared to inducing a certain recognition effect in the newcomer: Babylon – I'm sure I've heard that somewhere. Even at the airport there can be no doubt: in Vienna prostitution is everywhere, but it's decent, not at all conspicuous. The game of hide-and-seek is taken to perfection in Vienna.

In Vienna there is no world-famous red-light district like that in St. Pauli in Hamburg, and Vienna does not welcome its visitors with a sea of whorehouses like Frankfurt am Main. True, in Vienna, too, there are the bars along the Gürtel [the Belt], Vienna's main drag, close to the Westbahnhof [Railway Terminal West], and the streetwalker district just behind it, but these two sex-miles are more or less inconspicuous, at least compared with the massive presence of an official red-light district. In Vienna the visitor will not find a red-light district.

Spatial politics: Frankfurt am Main and Vienna compared

Frankfurt is famous – if not notorious – for its red-light district, the so-called Bahnhof [Railway Station] district. In the 1980s international investors, with the backing of Frankfurt's mayor Walter Wallmann, sought to ban prostitution from the Bahnhof district over the long run as a means of developing new land for banks and insurance companies, but the project failed. This is noteworthy in view of the fact that otherwise new high-rise construction in Frankfurt seldom runs up against any limits (see Rodenstein 2000).

Expert interviews and a documentation published by Cora Molloy, the spokeswoman of the sexworkers' association 'HWG' (1992) make it plain that the disputes over prostitution – like the debate on ethnic segregation – is in fact concerned with the issue of 'spatial diffusion or concentration'. In essence, the resistance to a ban on prostitution in Frankfurt's Bahnhof district is keyed to the assumption that a diffusion of brothels across the city would bring all of its citizens into uncontrolled contact with venal sex. Be they churches, sexworkers' associations, or planning authorities, everyone prefers to see hookers concentrated, and thus under control, in one place. Dealing with the Northern Ireland conflict, Allen Feldman (1997) describes the need for visibility if individuals are to be controlled through spatial arrangements. Here Catholics and Protestants settle (or are settled) in districts of their own. This enables the British army to use video cameras to collectively monitor entire population groups which, without this spatial segregation, would be impossible to distinguish in physical terms. However, this visibility for the state – and the spatial segregation it implies – is at the same time the condition required to render the two competing population groups invisible for one another. The fact that these groups, constructed as antagonistic, are unlikely to meet in the course of day-to-day life both gives rise to and consolidates never-ending constructions of prejudice.

In the past the Frankfurt municipal administration also considered the use of video cameras to monitor the red-light district around the railroad station. The final result of years of disputes between city-planning institutions, affected residents, churches, and international investors over whether to dissolve the district-specific structure of sexwork (as in Vienna) or to concentrate it in one quarter was to place the Bahnhof area, both symbolically and materially, on a new legal, planning, and social footing as Frankfurt's red-light district. What was finally established is a place of the Other (see Hubbard 1998). Just as sexworkers are constructed as the Other of the dominant heterosexual-patriarchal standard, so, Hubbard notes further, does the other become spatially visible in the red-light district. It would be possible to localize all conceivable negative attributes here, from filthy to violent and immoral, and to define one's own place, in contrast, as 'pure'. If we assume that identity is achieved via integration in spaces, then the act of demarcation can also be used for a sexualized construction of normality. The visibility of 'immorality', filth, and disease in the other district makes it possible to localize all this outside one's own lifeworld.

On every just about street corner in Vienna there are red-light bars with separate booths, sex movie theaters, swinger clubs, etc.; occasionally small concentrations may be found. At a conservative estimate of the police some 5000 women offer their services as sexworkers in Vienna. Only 460 of these women are legally registered to provide sex services. This figure is on the decline. In 1913, 1879 women were registered; in 1993 the figure was 711. If a woman (or a man) is registered in Vienna as a prostitute, she (he) is, in the jargon of the police and health authorities, referred to as a 'controlled prostitute' – as opposed to a 'clandestine prostitute'. There is some justification for the terminology. A registered sexworker is photographed and fingerprinted. Police officers from the relevant department are authorized to inquire at the sexworker's place of abode to determine whether her husband (or his wife) is unemployed and might possibly be engaged in procurement. If a woman works the streets, she is required to register for a fixed location.

Michel Foucault (1977) presents us with an exemplary analysis of how individuality is produced through localization and registration. One's own place, a specific designation, is the *sine qua non* for control and punishment. If a woman is found not to be at her place, she is liable to be fined. According to social workers, the level of these fines has been raised in recent years. Fines of between 150 and 900 euros, which are typical, are simply too high for the women affected. According to information provided by two counseling services, Lefö and Sila, the women most often fined are Nigerian. In this case racism and sexism may be seen going hand in hand.

Officially, there are no brothels in Vienna. The prostitution law, however, does permit women to work in dwellings that are used or lived in exclusively by persons engaged in prostitution, provided that the buildings [in question] have direct and separate access from a public street. These women are not allowed to work at home in their own dwellings.

On the ground: exploring the Belt

I start out with the brothels along the Belt. Today, the spatial arrangement is heterogeneous. The buildings around the subway station house scene bars, small booths where kebab is sold; and the alleyways are punctuated, at more or less regular intervals, by bars illuminated in red. Both the facades and the advertising are designed to give off stereotyped signals: The lips, the champagne glass, the high-heeled shoe. Again and again! A special kind of aesthetics is the central component to attract some and to exclude others. There is music in the air. And there are women standing in front of some of the bars. All with white skin, black getup, and red lips. Somehow they have all managed to be blond on this evening. Sometimes you see women sitting in shop windows.

Figure 4.2 Neonglas
Source: Author.

They don't move. Their legs are stretched upward, their heads tossed back. They seem relaxed, and very attractive. I go into a bar. It's still early in the evening. There are hardly any male customers to be seen. Coming in from the dusky light outside, I am overwhelmed by the darkness inside. I can hardly make out the arrangements. Visibility is reduced to a minimum. But there is an odor of sweetish perfume in the air. I was told by the feminist counseling centers that you have to ask the owner or the barmaid whether you can speak to the women there. It occurs to me that earlier older men asked the man accompanying me whether they could speak to, or indeed even dance with, me. Protection and patronage are seldom far apart. I walk up to a woman. For me, deciding which one to speak to is just as intuitive as the conduct of customers is always reported to be. Customers approach these women, and they in turn signal their readiness to respond openly. The women are not simply passively chosen. They use glances, poises to express sympathy or rejection. Many customers are – like me in this situation – very insecure. We are glad for the signals given by the women. Street workers tell stories about the concerns of a good number of sexworkers who are not often approached by men. For the most part – social workers report – women who despise their own activity have more trouble acquiring customers than women who think highly of, or are at least tolerant of, sexuality, their trade, or their own body. Indeed, a women doctor with the public health office is convinced that it is possible to distinguish two groups: women who, in one way or another, have developed a positive sense of sexuality and other women who are 'broken' by sexwork. The health examination is an intimate procedure. While many sexworkers are ashamed to take their place in the gynecological chair, others take the opportunity to embarrass the doctor by coming out with untoward sexualized utterances, i.e. by playing games with her. They use sexualized, lesbian innuendo to undercut medical authority.

So I approach the women whose gaze I interpret as curiosity and frankness. When I tell her that I am conducting research on prostitutions, she grins. Probably – it suddenly occurs to me – she is studying sociology. I'm glad that I'm not offering any seminars at the University of Vienna. But why is that?

What we are in here is an arrangement deliberately staged as 'another, a different world'. It's oppressively hot. Otherwise the women would be cold, lightly dressed as they are. The dominant colors are red and black. I speak with the sexworker about a concern allegedly often addressed by women, namely men. She tells me that men – at least those who are not regulars – always first sit down at the bar – and seek to survey the room. They often prefer to remain on their safe seat at the bar and have the women shown to them there – without having to walk through the room, exposing themselves to the gaze of the others. They prefer to gaze themselves. The barmaid helps out. 'Come on, show yourselves!' is a call frequently to be heard. This allows the man to gaze and choose.

Practice of visibility

Men don't want to be seen. Christine Howe, who worked for many years with the now-defunct prostitute project Agisra e.V., reports:

> We also do street work, and when you see how men start out by looking around before entering a brothel, you get the impression that their space-related threshold fear is also an endopsychic fear. When, on the other hand, you observe them leaving the brothel, sometimes even falling out the door and having to seek orientation, sometimes even walking off in the wrong direction, then it almost seems as though they had just stepped over the threshold between two completely different worlds. (Howe, quoted after Domentat 2003, 93f.)

As one social worker reports, taking a photo in the red-light district is like switching on the light. I don't know how often I have heard – slightly amused – insiders report that men tend look around before entering such a bar to make sure nobody is watching them. A brothel operator reports that many men hardly even have the courage to look these women straight in the eye.

As with any social encounter, the culture of the gaze is the essential element here that defines the opening of the encounter. The basis rule is that it is the women – not the men – who have to show themselves. That is, they stage a showing that veils their own gaze, giving the men a greater sense of security. One essential component of this enactment is to seem to cede the voyeuristic gaze to the man.

Studies on film theory and picture interpretation (for a summary, see Mathes 2001, 105; Hentschel 2001) suggest that practicing a scientifically detached viewing, for example, of paintings, is an approach used to produce and reproduce the cultural construction of heterosexuality. The picture based on perspective creates the impression of depth and thus of spatiality before the eyes of the beholder, a spatiality which is further reinforced by the moving pictures served up in the cinema.

> The commercial film aims, by employing inconspicuous cutting and camera techniques, to create the impression of a continuous, homogenous picture space and to place the observer in a panoramic position. (Hentschel 2001, 153)

The fact that spaces have traditionally been imagined as women('s bodies) (see Löw 2001, 115ff.; Löw 2006a for more information) gives rise to a cultural association between spaces viewed and female bodies. As literary criticism has frequently noted, this overlapping of spatial fantasies and female bodies (see Weigel 1990; Kubitz-Kramer 1995) ties the perspective-minded voyeuristic gaze, which dissects without being seen, into a genderized and genderizing context. In the absolutist notion of space the open pictorial space is experienced as something like the promise of a tender and open female body, and at the same time described as the womb with its promise of security (Colomina 1997) and of lust (Weigel 1990; Hentschel 2001). Against the background of a dual-gender, heterosexual matrix, two potentially contrary positions become manifest: that of the male gaze and that of the female as the object gazed upon.

Some brothel/bar operators manage to make optimal use of the potentials of the world of the image and the film. The encounters between men and women inside a bar, devised as it is to having women show themselves, places the man in a panoramic position. The women before his eyes move as if they were in a film – and these are women who are willing to keep the promise of the open female body, and who, using, say, makeup and wigs, shape their body in conformity with stereotyped images of femininity. The picture space is also reenacted through the arrangement of the show windows. Women place themselves in the window frame in such a way as to blur the difference between endless images of iniquitous women and a concrete bodily presence. The women become the picture by bodily practices and aesthetic performances. One thing that is typical here is that establishments that do not advertise by placing women in their windows often replace them with a picture. In astonishing monotony, the typical Viennese façade will feature a champagne glass and a high-heeled shoe as symbols of prostitution.

While the high-heeled shoe may be read as a fetish, the champagne glass suggests, to the pornographic gaze, the male organism (see Figure 4.2). The popping cork, the spurting champagne, are commonly staged as a symbol for male ejaculation and orgasm. The glass, with its triangular form resting on the stem, is designed to receive the champagne, with its associations of ejaculate. This set the stage for the inoffensive champagne glass on the façade to tell its tale of promise and well-being.

Figure 4.3 Tannengruen
Source: Jutta Güldenpfennig.

Comparing this with, for example, Frankfurt am Main, we find in Frankfurt that – apart from the stereotyped signals referred to above – these stagings are more clearly addressed to specific milieus. Here distinction is the principle behind the aesthetics. Here we find façade designs that include flowerboxes and fir sprigs that remind the observer of Christmas family idylls, and yet red lamps, supported by red ribbons in the fir sprigs, clearly indicate what the building contains. A clearly observable threshold enactment points unmistakably to the building's acquired public character as a brothel. Self-assured and openly sexualized, two oversized female legs, connected only by a lightly clad lower abdomen, represent the gateway to the world of sexwork.

Figure 4.4 Damenbeine
Source: Jutta Güldenpfennig.

Other buildings work with artful stagings, with show-window dummies, day and night, conveying to the outside, in various poses, what must be supposed to be happening inside. The figures awaken associations of movie scenes, and these façade decorations assume the character of art in public spaces. Every building has music of its own. While one brothel plays Grönemeyer's *Männer*, ironically parodying its own doings, in another, well-known Oktoberfest songs raise expectations of arrangements that have little to do with the atmosphere conjured up by classical piano sonatas.

Local differences, urban cultures, and national legislation

Despite a certain underlying deprecation and stigmatization of prostitutes as 'unrespectable!', voluntary prostitution has been a legal activity in Germany since the 1970s. Yet up to late 2001 deals concluded with prostitutes for sexual services were regarded both by relevant court decisions and by §138 of the German Civil Code as improper. One of the consequences was that deals and contracts on sexual services were not valid under civil law and were thus deemed null and void (see, for example, www.eu-puffs.de/rechtsstellung.shtml). The new German law on prostitution (the so-called Prostitution Law – ProstG) has meant an incisive change in the legal situation of prostitutes. The background was a legal dispute over a certain Café Pssst! whose owner had refused to register her affiliated guesthouse under a different name. The judge hearing the case, Percy Maclean, queried 50 socially relevant groups and individuals – church representatives, scientists, associations, labor unions, etc. – on their opinions on sex-related transactions. The majority of these witnesses

> saw nothing improper in prostitution, exercised in free responsibility and without any accompanying criminal activities, and soberly stated that voluntarily provided sexual services must be regarded as a social reality if they do not collide with the penal code or the law on the protection of minors. (Domentat 2003: 30f.)

In other words, today prostitution is no longer improper.

This new self-image of Germany's sex industry – which preceded the new law and is at the same time its product – finds expression in the shape given to public space. Striking installations, façade designs, decorations are used to address and to distinguish customer groups. An additional factor in Frankfurt as compared with Vienna is that here the business is structured more by big companies and large-scale brothels or publicly accessible sex centers in which prostitution is clearly recognizable as work, while in Vienna it is more typical for a small group to operate one or more smaller-scale brothels.

In Frankfurt this makes it possible for brothel complexes that include several houses to develop corporate identities of their own, while in Vienna the strategy is more to stick with the use of recurrent and proven symbols. Due to a certain uniformity and smallness found in the Vienna scene, the spaces of prostitution play less of a role as an element contributing to the shaping of public space, and may perhaps be compared to fluorescent strips: perceptible, but elusive. That is to say, it is both national legal elements and city-specific economic networks and urban cultural specifics that shape prostitution in its spatio-social aspects.

Is it chance that it is precisely in the city of Vienna that this dynamic of inconspicuous showing is the key formal element in play: a city famed both for its façades and for the avant-garde architecture of an Adolf Loos, with its bare, white walls; a city in which people are unwilling to live in ground-floor apartments because passers-by might be able to look in and see them? Certainly not! Vienna lacks a 'place of the other' that is at once visible for all and familiar to every child. Vienna has many, scattered places of the other that together form a space of their own, those refer to and complement one another. In Vienna people still tell the story of Kaiser Joseph II, who, asked to lift the ban on brothels, is said to have responded, 'What, brothels? All I'd have to do is build a big roof over the whole of Vienna...' (Anwander and Neudecker 1999, 67).

So it is that the structure of the trade reproduces itself at the city level. The game of hide-and-seek, a favorite of modern society, is perfected in sexwork. Both social workers and customers report again and again on the 'other world' that they encounter in relevant bars. Many of them have trouble describing this other world. In interviews they refer to it as 'mysterious' or note that 'it's the clandestine that shapes the atmosphere'. If they are to survive, secrets may not be allowed to become public. In the field of prostitution male customers and sexworkers/'clandestine prostitutes' work hand in hand in preserving the secretive, mysterious. Women who are not part of paid sexwork are simply members of the bothersome public. Prostitution reverses the middle-class logic that assigns women to the private sphere and opens up a subcultural field of public female bodies (the prostitutes) and a public sphere, which is then the sphere of 'middle-class' women.

But what is it that is enacted here as a secret meant to be kept? Male sexuality? Sexuality in general? Male insecurity? Few studies have been written on male customers. And these are based on reports of prostitutes, not on what customers themselves have to say (Girtler 1990, 143ff.; Bilitewski *et al*. 1994/1991). There is little founded information available on the films – including films of different types – in which men set out to play the leading role by setting foot in a brothel. It is a striking fact that (surprisingly) many elements of the love film crop up in the world of anonymous sex. 'Ring the bell and step into bliss', announces one sign on the door of a Vienna brothel. Others place little hearts and arrows in clearly visible spots of the entryway, or use neon signs blinking out the call 'Love me'.

In an interview study, Sabine Grenz (2005, 162) shows how important it is for many men not be nagged by the sense that 'it' is all done for the money. And if it still feels that way, these men tend to believe that they have simply not paid enough. Despite this explicit 'the more expensive, the more genuine' logic, many men are convinced that their favorite whore is really happy to see them in person; that a domina is a woman who really likes to deal out blows; or that 'certain reactions' show them that there are 'things [that] you just can't fake' (Grenz 2005, 163). The ideal of the private relationship, Grenz notes, assumes an unadulterated form in prostitution: an exchange based on give and take. 'In Germany over one million men avail themselves daily of the services [provided by prostitutes]' (Deutscher Bundestag 2001, 4; see also Laskowski 1997, 80). The Berlin Hydra prostitute self-help-project even estimates that every day up to 1.5 million men make use of the services of prostitutes (see Mitrovic 2002, 70).

In this connection, the definitions of prostitution typically offered by the social sciences may be 'summed up as "sex for money" with various modifications' (Laskowski 1997, 46). Accordingly, prostitutes are referred to as persons or 'individuals who receive payment (whether financial or otherwise) for sexual services' (Hubbard 1998, 269). Only sound consumer research would be able to determine whether or not this definition does not more than oversimplify the field of prostitution. It is likely that in the end no secrets will be revealed; instead, the enactment of the secret opens up the possibility to step across a threshold. Nothing happens on the other side that is not concealed by the one side as well, but the enactment of an 'other side' opens up fantasy spaces, shifts in the staging and practices of desire. Furthermore, it is precisely the enactment of the male and the female as its object – a far more fragile experience in everyday life – that is used to learn and practice a basic social structure that serves to stabilize power relations, as it were despite the fragility of everyday experience.

On the ground: exploring roadside prostitution

Another striking difference between Vienna and Frankfurt am Main is the dimensions of and the major role played by roadside prostitution in Vienna. The ban there on brothels has made streetwalker districts the main scene of the trade. The upper Mariahilfer Strasse, including the side streets around it as well as the area surrounding the Prater and the fairgrounds, are the most important of them. As Georg Simmel (1995, 780ff.) noted, access to and affiliation with a house implies a tie to a community and thus serves to forge an imaginary closed unit. On the other hand, the practice of standing out on the street serves to localize prostitutes as individuals. Women standing in front of Belt brothels can be seen leaning against the wall of the brothel in which they work. Women who work in the area of the Mariahilfer Strasse stand along the front edge of the sidewalk. They seem unsupported without the immediate backing of solid building walls. The act of stepping forward brings these women into an unstable spatial situation of exposure, leaving them unprotected on all sides. At the same time, they are engaged in an activity recognizable as a public function. In her study *Klandestine Welten. Mit Goffmann auf dem Drogenstrich*, Antje Langer (2003) compares this stepping forward with a theatrical performance:

> By separating from her group and taking up her position, for all to see, at the side of the street, she has stepped out on to the forestage. The customers, driving and strolling around, can now perceive her as a prostitute and thus include her in their interactions (Langer 2003, 83).

Accordingly, the individual prostitute uses this act of stepping forward, also an act of showing oneself, both as a means of shifting her mode of staging and of defining a difference between the woman offering her services and the woman who just happens to be there at the time. The latter factor is also underlined by the working clothes worn on the occasion – at least if the prostitution in question is procurement-related. Individuality is blurred by leather and latex, high-heeled shoes, and blond or black wigs. Many women working along Mariahilfer Strasse also make use of this principle of marketing. Most, though, stand along the sidewalk in jeans and running shoes. Those standing on street corners in casual clothing and carrying a handbag are all of African descent. Being a Nigerian woman in Vienna is evidently marketing enough.

On my explorations along Mariahilfer Strasse I myself am always dressed inconspicuously. It is cold. I wear a long coat and flat-heeled shoes. I walk as if I were headed for a goal, and without establishing eye contact with the cars passing by. Even so, innumerable cars stop beside me. Many of these potential customers, old and young, drivers of cheap and expensive cars, can inevitably be found again waiting at the next intersection. As soon as I approach the intersection, they roll down their window (sometimes just pushing the button).

How is it possible that numerous and systematic 'misunderstandings' are part and parcel of a field so clearly governed in its system of interaction by positionings, stagings of the body, and eye context? Most of the protests made by adjacent residents are directed at traffic-related noise pollution and the constant propositions made to women living in the area. According to Antje Langer, a larger, probably the largest, group of men circle around the block with the intention not of playing a role as customers but of observing events from the perspective of the voyeur.

> The voyeurs don't need the signals given off by the prostitutes, since they are driven by motives other than communication and sexual contact with these women. For these men, distance, in the sense of disregard, is simply not a concern. They ignore women's attempts to draw a line between them, attempts that I would understand as a clear-cut demonstration that these women are not part of the ensemble of prostitution. Demonstrations of this kind may e.g. include external appearances, like clothing that differs clearly from that worn by the sexworkers or the fact that an observer is pushing a bicycle. [...] Male companions, who in many other public places are able to protect women from overly obvious and obtrusive glances and comments [...] have no such luck with many motorized customers. (Langer 2003: 85)

In many streets and districts that have been legalized for prostitution, or are simply used for the purpose, effects are generated through the creation of this one, specific place. The way in which such places are symbolically charged serves to suspend the local validity of fundamental forms of social interaction such as gender-specific rules governing approach and distance, greeting rituals and contact practices. The place and the spaces constituting it are set as dominant in relation to social conventions otherwise regarded as normal. Forced to comprehend the spatial arrangements involved in living and in prostitution as different approaches to structuring social space (see Löw 2001; 2006b), many customers take the opportunity to confirm the existence of a space of the Other as constitutive. Consistently, the authorities responsible for law and order use space-related strategies to respond to the protests of adjacent residents; for example, they constantly alter the direction of one-way streets to shake up the spatial regimes, as in Vienna's Stuwer district.

Conclusions

In the field of prostitution, femininity is on the one hand enacted in an ideal-typical fashion, while on the other hand, and in many different ways, traditional gender roles are 'broken' (though without being invalidated), for example, by the fact that women are paid for relationship or sex work and by the protective space created to deal with male insecurities, including a legitimization of impotence. Embedded in a culture of the brothel, men's systematic attempts at concealment are bought at the expense of women having to show themselves. In certain segments of prostitution the heterosexual matrix of the male gaze and the female role as the object of the gaze is perfected in an overlap of women and image, thus confirming the distanced and distancing panorama position held by men. The encounters between men and women are organized by bodily practices and aesthetic performances: the women become the picture.

The tension between private and public, in its historical genesis closely intertwined with the Western two-gender regime, is specifically (re)produced in the field of sexwork. Even though today women in public spaces are no longer generally suspected of prostitution, the symbolic surplus of the place is stronger than the socially negotiated interaction regime. At the same time, we find in the brothel a reversal of the middle-class logic that ties women to the private sphere, one that opens up a subcultural field consisting of public female bodies (the prostitutes) and a locked-out public sphere, i.e. the marginalization of all women not engaged in prostitution.

As a voluntary sexual service, prostitution is generally legal, even though it is, in a complex and in particular spatially differentiated form, legally regimented and, as far as its spatial and gender-related arrangements are concerned, the taint of 'immorality or impropriety' continues even today to operate as a factor of social distinction. The field is organized as a genderized field through *spacing* practices, i.e. the placing of objects and persons (and thus of the body), as well as through *synthesizing* acts on the basis of which spaces are perceived as specific, symbolically charged, and interrelated elements.

And last but not least, my comparison of Vienna and Frankfurt am Main has pointed to the analytical significance of urban cultures. The cognitive interest in the heterogeneity of cities and the conditions under which people live in them vanished, in particular in German-language urban studies, together with the difference between town and country and the worldwide onslaught of practically indistinguishable commodities, symbols, and pictures. This we see in particular in the assumption that, irrespective of local contextual conditions, the course of sociation is the same for the nation-state and for world society – with differences, if there are any in the first place, expressed in terms of, say, a city's financial importance (global city research). One exception here is the field of historical science, which, while contributing numerous '(hi)stories' of individual cities, and enlarging our knowledge of the historical nature and status of cities, has nevertheless seldom focused comparatively on structural relations. Both approaches thus look into urban processes and generalize the results of their analyses to the level of the conditions obtaining for society as a whole. In a manner that at first may seem paradoxical, the logic of research has led to the invention of the 'city' as a homogeneous whole, a practice that reproduces the assumption of homogeneity from the global level down to the urban level. At the same time, and as it were against the thrust of the ample research data available on homogenization, observation of sexwork comes up with locally specific arrangements of a field that appears at the global level and is legally regulated at the national level. If we look at the city merely as a (random) setting for specific research, or if we unquestioningly equate urban structures with modern social structures, we lose sight of the locally different material structures, lifestyles, aesthetics and narratives of a homogenizing urban reality.

References

Anwander, B. and Neudecker, S. (1999), *Sex in Wien* (Wien: Falter Verlag).

Bilitewsky, H. *et al.* (Prostituiertenprojekt Hydra) (eds) (1991/1994), *Freier. Das heimliche Treiben der Männer* (Hamburg: Galgenberg Verlag).

Colomina, B. (1997), 'Die gespaltene Wand: häuslicher Voyeurismus', in Kravagna, C. (ed.).

Deutscher Bundestag – 14.Wahlperiode (2001), *Begründung des Gesetzes zur Regelung der Rechtsverhältnisse der Prostituierten* Drucksache 14/5958, 4–6.

Domentat, T. (2003), *,Laß dich verwöhnen'. Prostitution in Deutschland* (Wien: Aufbau Verlag).

Feldman, A. (1997), 'Violence and Vision: The Prosthetics and Aesthetics of Terror', *Public Culture* 10:1, 24–60.

Foucault, M. (1977), *Discipline and Punish: The Birth of the Prison* (London: Allen Lane).

Girtler, R. (1990), *Der Strich. Sexualität als Geschäft* (Wien: LIT Verlag).

Grenz, S. (2005), *(Un)heimliche Lust. Über den Konsum sexueller Dienstleistungen* (Wiesbaden: VS Verlag).

Hentschel, L. (2001), 'Die Ordnung von Raum und Geschlecht in der visuellen Kultur des 19. und 20. Jahrhunderts', in Krüger, M. and Wallisch-Prinz, B. (eds).

Hubbard, P. (1998), 'Sexuality, Immorality and the City. Red-light Districts and the Marginalisation of Female Prostitutes', *Gender, Place and Culture* 5:1, 55–76.

Kravagna, C. (ed.), *Privileg Blick. Kritik der visuellen Kultur* (Berlin: Edition ID-Archiv).

Krüger, M. and Wallisch-Prinz, B. (eds), *Erkenntnisprojekt Feminismus* (Bremen: Donat).

Kublitz-Kramer, M. (1995), *Frauen auf Straßen. Topographien des Begehrens in Erzähltexten von Gegenwartsautorinnen* (Munich: W. Fink Verlag).

Langer, A. (2003), *Klandestine Welten. Mit Goffman auf dem Drogenstrich* (Königstein: Ulrike Helmer Verlag).

Laskowski, R.S. (1997), *Die Ausübung der Prostitution. Ein verfassungsrechtlich geschützter Beruf im Sinne von Art. 12 Abs.1 GG* (Frankfurt am Main: Peter Lang Verlag).

Löw, M. (2001), *Raumsoziologie* (Frankfurt am Main: Suhrkamp Verlag).

Löw, M. (2006a), 'The Social Construction of Space and Gender', accepted for publication in *European Journal of Women's Studies* 13:2.

Löw, M. (2006b), 'The Double Existence of Space as Structural Ordering and Action', accepted for publication in *Travaux de l'Institut de Geographie de Reims* (TIGR).

Mathes, B. (2001), *Verhandlungen mit Faust. Geschlechterverhältnisse in der Kultur der Frühen Neuzeit* (Königstein: Ulrike Helmer Verlag).

Mitrovic, E. (2002), 'Frauenarbeitsplatz Prostitution. Arbeitsbedingungen in einem bedeutenden Wirtschaftsfaktor' *Forum Wissenschaft* 1, 70–73.

Molloy, C. (1992), *Hurenalltag. Sperrgebiet – Stigma – Selbsthilfe. Materialien zur Sozialarbeit und Sozialpolitik,* Band 34 (Frankfurt am Main: Schriftenreihe der Fachhochschule Frankfurt am Main).

Rodenstein, M. (ed.) (2000), *Hochhäuser in Deutschland: Zukunft oder Ruin der Städte?* (Stuttgart: Kohlhammer Verlag).

Simmel, G. (1995), *Soziologie. Untersuchungen über die Formen der Vergesellschaftung. Gesamtausgabe Band II* (Frankfurt am Main: Suhrkamp Verlag).

Weigel, S. (1990), *Topographien der Geschlechter. Kulturgeschichtliche Studien zur Literatur* (Reinbek: Rowohlt Verlag).

Internet-based references

'Die Rechtsstellung von Prostituierten', <http://www.eu-puffs.de/rechtsstellung.shtml>, accessed 30 April 2006.

This article was translated by Paul Knowlton.

Chapter 5

Urban Spaces Re-Defined in Daily Practices – 'Minibar', Ankara[1]

Deniz Altay

Introduction – discussions on urban space

The aim of this article is to emphasize that an important amount of information is disguised within the daily life of the city. This argument depends firstly on a specific position taken in the investigation of urban life and space that puts the urban researcher among the urban inhabitants, not detached from them. Secondly, it derives from the assertion that the 'ordinary practitioners of the city' (de Certeau 1984, 93) have the capacity to produce their own spaces. This implies that the urban space is also a 'social construct' (Massey 1993, 145); and it is perpetually produced through the socio-spatial practices of the city dwellers.

Advancing from this approach, urban researchers are ready to encounter a multiplicity of urban phenomena, which will open beyond them a wide area of investigation. This study accordingly suggests the investigation of urban space as a tool and medium for obtaining actual knowledge on the inhabitant, the society, and wider cultural, economic, sociological, and political processes.

Developed around this primary concern, this article is based on a research, which elaborated an urban phenomenon that is taking place in the city of Ankara. 'Minibar', as anonymously named by its participants, is a space created by a group of young people through the performance of a leisure activity: drinking on the street and being with friends.

If one is to walk without purpose the Tunalı Hilmi Avenue in Ankara on a warm Saturday evening, one will drift along the lively crowd on the avenue, embraced by people moving from shops to cafés, from cafés to cinemas, from parks to their home, and one may easily fall in the middle of the lively Minibar crowds, in the back streets of 'Tunalı'. Passing by a street crossing the Tunalı Hilmi Avenue, one can encounter scattered groups of people who hang out in the street, just as in Figure 5.1. Minibar

---

1   This article is based on research conducted by the author during 2003–2004, at Middle East Technical University, Faculty of Architecture.

takes place in one of the important central areas of Ankara. It is the story of young people's nights of fun, of the residents discontents, and of the struggle between them; and consequently of the continuous change taking place in the neighborhood.

Figure 5.1
Source: Can Altay, *Minibar Photograph Series*, 2002–2003.

Accepting the possibility of the 'space of the inhabitant' in the city means accepting the possibility of a multiplicity of ways of defining and producing space (Lefebvre 1991). Within a quick account, spaces are firstly defined in the words and thoughts, in the visions and programs of the professionals. Spaces get restricted in the budgets, manipulated by the objectives of investors, and consequently spaces are constructed and provided to the use of the inhabitants. Then, as it is asserted in this study, spaces are re-defined in the daily lives, practices and acts, in the imagination and creativity of the urban dwellers and visitors.

Accordingly, it is these spatial experiences that complete the definition of the urban space. In this article, it is emphasized that the urban environment is also produced in practices, in the ways inhabitants 'use' it. The idea of such a production is based on Michel de Certeau's works. In *The Practice of Everyday Life*, where he questions the ways in which users operate, he suggests that the process of using is not, as it is commonly assumed, 'passive and guided by established rules' (de Certeau 1984, xi). Creativity is hidden in the way products are used (de Certeau 1984, xii, xiii), and in 'what the consumer *makes* or *does*' (de Certeau 1984, xii) with the product. If we adapt a similar perspective for the built environment, the urban space will be introduced as the product of both the 'designers' and the city dwellers. If planning, design, and construction are the first steps of this production; then use, experience, and appropriation are the following steps of it, composing the un-planned and unpredictable phase of using.

Attributing a productive capacity to the way the built environment is used; an investigation about 'urban spaces re-defined in daily practices' should recognize, above all, that the urban users have different ways of understanding and experiencing the city compared to the professionals or the institutions that set the definitions of urban space and that materially produce the built environment. Partly because of this difference of understanding and partly because of their particular needs and desires, the inhabitants seek to manipulate the urban environment in their own way; and this, within the approach of the study, is considered to be the first and primary stimulus for the appropriation of the urban environment which is already constructed and in use.

When the city inhabitants start to use the urban space in their own ways and through their own perspectives they start to re-define it to produce their own space. This approach introduces the urban space as composed of those provided places, which are in perpetual re-formation within the daily practices of the inhabitants. The practice of the inhabitant that is mentioned here is part of the daily routine; therefore not necessarily deliberately developed for the production of a space. On the contrary the re-defined space is an unintended production. Not planned, not calculated, not widely contemplated upon; but only frequented, experienced, lived; appropriated, interpreted, and manipulated through the needs and desires of the inhabitants.

The idea of urban space as practiced by the inhabitants depends on Henri Lefebvre's theories on *The Production of Space* and the triad of spatiality[2] he introduced. Thought within his inspiring approach, the 're-defined space' is neither like the space in the conceptualizations of the 'designer' – the representations of space, nor like the space that is materially constructed and produced – spatial practices; but it is the space as it is actually experienced and lived. The space of representation[3] is significant in this respect being the space 'as directly lived through its associated images and symbols, and hence the space of the "inhabitants" and "users".' (Lefebvre 1991, 39)

The case of Minibar

The case of Minibar is significant within this frame as an urban space that is used and appropriated by a group of young people. The research on the case of Minibar

2   Lefebvre formulates a tripartite understanding of (social) space (Lefebvre 1991, 33), comprising three moments that are connected to each other: spatial practices – perceived space; representations of space – concieved space; and representational spaces – lived space (Lefebvre 1991, 38–9).

3   The term 'spaces of representation' is used by Borden, Kerr, Pivaro, Rendell (2001) in place of representational spaces with the aim of providing a clearer understanding of the original concept introduced by Lefebvre.

initially aims to develop an understanding of urban space as appropriated through the inhabitants' particular ways of using it; and accordingly of the ways in which they create their own spaces within the built environment. Moreover, it discusses whether there are possible ways for the inhabitant groups to represent and express themselves through the spaces they produce.

With this prospect, the research comprises an in-depth interview study realized with the Minibar participants.[4] The interview study questions the production and use of Minibar by asking the participants about their experiences and opinions. The interviews have been evaluated based on Grounded Theory Analysis.[5]

Minibar takes place in the streets adjacent to a central avenue in Ankara, the Tunalı Hilmi Avenue, in the Kavaklıdere district. Neighborhoods of higher socio-economic profile surround this district as analyzed in the income/status study of Ankara (Guvenç 2001). There are cultural and commercial activities along this avenue, including a large number of food, beverage, and leisure establishments. Although at first glance Minibar seems to be a crowd in front of these places, it is a crowd of scattered youth groups who do not necessarily enter these places, but who come to the district for nightlife activity.

'Minibar' sounds at first like the name of a bar; but it is neither a formally established bar, nor a nightclub. However, as the name indicates, it is strongly associated with alcohol. Bottles of beer, in the hands of young boys and girls, are one sign of encountering Minibar in the streets of Ankara. Furthermore, the place called Minibar is not a covered or closed place. It is an outside space or a place outside. As the artist Can Altay explains:[6] 'The provided space is not an interior of a defined space. The Minibar is located in an in-between space; a gap; literally the space between the buildings.' (Altay 2003, 161)

The origin of the word 'Minibar' is unknown to most of its users; only the initiators know how the name came to be used. But once it was spoken out loud, every member of the group and then every newcomer accepted it. Minibar was initially the name given to the streets where groups of young people 'hang out' as a night activity; but in time it became the name given for both the space being created and the practice performed there: 'doing Minibar'.

According to the interviews made with the Minibar participants, the practice of Minibar is primarily defined by drinking outside on the street with friends. Eight years ago, Minibar had begun as a drinking stop in front of a grocery shop that was open until late at night. As it is prohibited to enter a night place with drinks bought

---

4   The population of Minibar varies in different seasons of the year, in different days of the week, in different hours of the day; Minibar does not have a constant population. Its peak moments are spring and summer weekends, before the holiday season begins, starting from the evening hours until late at night. Depending on the observations made in the field at such nights, Minibar population increased up to seventy people or even more.

5   For further reading see Arksey and Knight 1999; Charmaz 2003; Esterberg 2001.

6   'The Minibar Projections', installation: *How Lattitudes Become Forms: Art in a Global Age,* Walker Art Center, Minneapolis – USA (2003); *Fondazione Sandretto Re Rebaudengo per l'Arte*, Turin – Italy (2003); Contemporary Art Museum, Houston – USA (2004).

from elsewhere, small groups of bar clientele gathered in the street and bought cheaper drinks from the grocery shop before or after going to the bars. Hence they carried their leisure outdoors and invented Minibar. The reasons behind the initiation and the popularity of Minibar are above all the cheaper beverage prices in the grocery shops, having friends around, and the lively conversations on the street.

The participants of Minibar are composed of separate groups of friends. The groups comprise both male and female participants of ages between 16 to 27, most of them high school and university students or university graduates; coming from middle or high income families; yet very few of them are working, so they are economically dependent upon their families. The Minibar gatherings happen spontaneously, as expressed by the participants, by the coming together of friend groups, within whom there is no apparent and intended organization.

The re-definition of urban spaces through the daily practices of the inhabitants

Minibar is introduced in this study as a re-defined space: there is no previous definition set for Minibar; it does not exist in the plans that have been developed so far. It is defined within the practice of its users and has no predictability. Hence it is not something or some place known; it is something or some place invented or discovered. It is invented within the inhabitants' alternative ways of using the city space and participants define it with reference to these practices.

This definition of Minibar, as explained by the participants, includes firstly and without exception the act of 'drinking on the street', outside, in open air. The second and the most important characteristic of this act is 'to be with friends'. The interviewees explain that this social aspect of Minibar usually comes above consumption and it is also a major component that defines that space. The friendly atmosphere, the opportunity to chat easily, to be open to all kinds of encounters, in other words the social aspect is the first point that differentiates Minibar from any other bar or nightclub. In Figure 5.2, we can see a lively and crowded Minibar gathering, where boys and girls are chatting all together. As explained in the interviews, participants come to Minibar to be with their friends, to meet new people, and to be able to talk while drinking. This is not possible in bars and nightclubs due to the crowd, loud music, noise, and the dark atmosphere.

Figure 5.2
Source: Can Altay, *Minibar Photograph Series*, 2002–2003.

Minibar participants define the act also with reference to the streets where it is performed as a practice. The act, and the crowds of Minibar, are mainly dispersed on to two streets within the Kavaklıdere district. The district is specific for Minibar's creation because, first, it is the center of leisure the Minibar participants prefer to frequent. This is an important factor in Minibar's initiation in this district, yet Minibar increased the attractiveness of the area and in time, influenced the opening of new places for leisure. Kavaklıdere is also the center of preference for the majority of the participants in their commercial and cultural activities, and further it is an important transportation node within the city. Although the creation of Minibar is related to the district, the spaces of Minibar are also related to the practice itself. Minibar may be created whenever and wherever a group of friends comes together and perform this leisure practice.

Historically, the district was planned with a majority of residential uses, and has been developing with an accelerating pace since the 1950s. In time, the city center expanded towards this part of the town (Bademli 1986, Altaban 1986). With little change in the building stock, the residential uses turned into commercial and office ones. Today Kavaklıdere is an extension of the Central Business District, where residential and commercial uses are mixed. Within this development, the neighborhood became an important leisure center in the city, attracting a great number of people. Although the residents of this neighborhood are now familiar with the nightlife practices, the development of Minibar as a practice, was unforeseen and did not have any previously assigned space.

The commercial establishments like bars formally appropriated parts of the residential neighborhood by using the tools of the property market and the existing building stock. On the other hand, Minibar, by pursuing an alternative leisure activity, appropriates the under-used elements of the city in ways which are inventive and unpredicted. Minibar temporarily occupies the gaps between buildings like the walls, pavements, stairs, and parking lots; and produces its ephemeral spaces; as shown in Figure 5.3. Then we can see that the leisure activity of a youth group is what creates the alternative spaces of Minibar. It is the perpetual practice of this new use that re-defines the space; and it is the excitement of encountering it and the demand for it that continuously attracts new populations to Minibar.

Figure 5.3
Source: Can Altay, *Minibar Photograph Series*, 2002–2003.

The alternative use introduced by the Minibar participants is an alternative socio-spatial practice which is performed during certain times, at certain places – places that already had a pre-defined use and function for themselves. The participants of Minibar, in de Certeau's terms, accept the given urban space and, 'turning it to their advantage' (de Certeau 1984, 30), 'metaphorize' (de Certeau 1984, 32) it. Therefore, the re-definition of a space implies an act of making, an 'operation' which is conducted through the specific ways of using and which includes a creative interpretation of the already organized space.

The peculiar new way through which the inhabitants use the urban space includes a creative and productive act. This is an operation as de Certeau formulates (1984: xii). This is also an 'architectural action' as defined by Gausa: an effect of expressing, operating, executing, and doing (2003, 26). Minibar, in spite of seeking for constructed structures, abstracts itself from the urban space and turns into an act. It becomes the 'act of doing Minibar', the act of creating a space; transient, temporary, mobile; an act implied by a new way of using urban space. Minibar becomes a micro space created by that act, in other words the spaces where this act is performed. Now, it can be anywhere in the city, in any city. Minibar is thus an act of production for the participants; an act of making a space of their own through their practices and which fits their particular needs.

Spatial characteristics of Minibar

The description of Minibar by its participants includes in general terms the streets where Minibar usually takes place, yet this lacks any specification about where it starts and where it ends. Minibar spatializes itself by appropriating the already existing urban setting, by using the existing urban elements as parts of its own spatiality. Minibar re-interprets them, applies different meanings and exercises different uses on them to construct its own space. Figure 5.4 is an instance from Minibar, where the participants are sitting on the pavements and chatting.

Figure 5.4
Source: Can Altay, *Minibar Photograph Series*, 2002–2003.

The way Minibar appropriates urban space is similar to what Iain Borden formulates as 'body-architecture' in his works on the practice of skateboarding (1998, 2001). He explains that at the heart of skateboarding lies the 'combination and re-combination of body, image, thought, action' (1998, 197). The architecture of skateboarding is in one way closer to the realm of the user and to the experience of a creation of space through bodily processes. As Borden explains, skateboarding initiated the re-interpretation of schoolyards, drained swimming pools and re-configured them as elementary parts of its own practice, assigning new meanings to them and producing a super-architectural space through the mentioned interaction of body, board, and terrain.

The appropriation of the 'left-over' elements of the street, in the sense Borden asserts, defines the spaces of Minibar temporarily. Both Minibar and street skating enter into a transient interaction with the urban elements provided by the street. Whereas this interaction depends more on the bodily performance of the skaters in the case of skateboarding, it is less performance-based in Minibar in this respect and depends more on the presence of the Minibar participants.

This way of interaction introduces the participants themselves as one of the major elements of Minibar's spatiality. The participants construct the urban space first through appropriating the walls, parking lots, stairs, and pavements; and second through their presence in the area: Minibar is inscribed on to the streets as a place that can be encountered. The young people themselves, with bottles and plastic glasses and standing against on the walls construct the spaces of Minibar, as seen in Figure 5.5. So when the Minibar crowd moves, when people leave, Minibar disappears. Hence the practice of Minibar gets spatialized temporarily. When the night is over for the Minibar participants, the street is left to its previous state. As one of the participants says: '[…] when people leave there is nothing left'.[7]

Figure 5.5
Source: Can Altay, *Minibar Photograph Series*, 2002–2003.

---

7   Quoted from the interviews realized and translated by Deniz Altay, 2004.

The spatiality of Minibar is different in many ways from a constructed, materialized space. It is an impermanent spatiality. It appropriates but it does not persist. It does not produce a durable physical structure. There is no constructed boundary separating the micro spaces of Minibar from the street. It has transparent fringes which can easily change form and which do not distinguish outside from inside. In fact there is no outside and inside. Minibar is diffused into the streets of Tunalı, filling the leftover, in-between spaces without forming any disclosure, and without isolating itself.

The micro spaces produced through the temporary acts of the Minibar users may change in form and position. This depends on the spontaneous decisions of the participants and on temporary conditions. Minibar is not fixed on the city space: it is an impermanent space. The perpetually re-defined spaces of Minibar are able to change location due to weather conditions, the interventions of the neighborhood residents or the intervention of the police. Whatever the external restraints are, Minibar is a mobile space, and may use this mobility in response.

Figure 5.6
Source: Can Altay, *Minibar Photograph Series*, 2002–2003.

Spaces produced by the inhabitants in their daily practices take the established urban space by appropriating it. When the inhabitants free themselves from the imposed rules, they start to develop their own ways of making space. That is why their operation can also be accepted as a tactical one. As de Certeau explains, the place where tactic operates 'belongs to the other' (1984, xix) and, he adds, a tactic, not having a proper place, depends on time: 'It must constantly manipulate events in order to turn them into "opportunities".' (de Certeau 1984, xix) The tactical operation of the inhabitant does not seek to change or re-construct the urban space; it only interprets the urban space in a peculiar, un-thought way and brings an additional definition to it. Unlike the durable constructions within the built environment, the alternative spaces of the user, reached through tactical operations, are ephemeral.

The micro spaces of Minibar are able to move, increase or decrease in size, emerge or disappear any time. Being a temporary act, Minibar does not need to build and construct to assure its continuity. On the contrary, it is the ephemerality of the practice which allows Minibar to repeat itself in time; because Minibar is neither as a practice nor as a space supported by the legal frame. It is unplanned, unforeseen, and it does not depend on formal regulations. Within these terms, the act of Minibar will come to an end if it seeks a permanent place for the performance of its practice.

Rivalry relations

The temporary operations and ephemeral occupations of the inhabitants, as in the case of Minibar and in the example of skateboarders given by Borden, comprise the introduction of a new way of using the urban space. With this new use continuously practiced on the streets, the user group achieves to open up its own space through 'infiltrating' (Morales 2003, 341) the urban environment.

The limits separating Minibar from the existing space are not clear, yet one is generated in spite of the other. Minibar, in a way, questions the limits that define urban space; and re-formulates it for its own spatiality. By doing so, Minibar 'tests the limits' (Doron 2003) and regulations of the established space in physical, social and legal terms but does not actually break them. In these terms, Minibar is a transgressive act.

Transgression, as Foucault (1977) explains, includes 'actions that are based on temporality, on testing limits and opening up new boundaries.' (Doron 2003) The concept of transgression opens up new possibilities for the discussion of marginal practices like Minibar by introducing an un-defined zone within which these practices can be exercised. 'Transgression is an action which involves the limit, that narrow zone of a line where it displays the flash of its passage, but perhaps also its entire trajectory, even its origin; it is likely that transgression has its entire space in the line it crosses.' (Foucault 1977, 33–4) The act of Minibar transgresses the limits of the imposed order, in the way it infiltrates and inserts a different order into it. It transgresses but it does not attack to damage the existing order. The Minibar practitioners temporarily occupy the urban space and they do not claim any legal right over it. They create their own order by pushing the existing limits back and forth. Nonetheless, the unpredicted activity of Minibar affects the other users of the vicinity.

The alternative space created by the practice of Minibar is not necessarily accepted and supported by every user. Consequently this unconformity initiates tensions among the users of the space when they encounter with each other. Different users of the area struggle to preserve the limits within which the urban environment and activity is defined. Within these limits, their properties and their professional, domestic, or social lives are regulated and protected. They struggle and they pro-act to the extent they feel uncomfortable, insecure, or threatened.

Minibar gets different reactions from different groups at the location, such as the passers-by, the neighborhood residents, the shop owners, the police, and so on. The major complaints come from the residents. For them, Minibar is a disturbing crowd generating noise and waste. Thus, the participants explain that the residents have developed ways to counteract their practices.

The tactical counter-operation of the residents includes methods like making loud spoken warnings from the windows such as 'please leave', or throwing water onto the Minibar participants. The most common warning they make is calling the police. The residents also make spatial manipulations, for example fortifying their territories to defend their area. They spread lime powder on the pavements or raise their front walls by putting fences on them to prevent people from sitting there. Figure 5.7 is an example of fences that have been put on a garden wall where Minibar participants frequently used to sit.

Figure 5.7
Source: Can Altay, *Minibar Photograph Series*, 2002–2003.

The participants accept the residents' preventive and defensive acts as their means of expressing discontent. Similar to the way the Minibar practice questions the limits of the existing space; neighborhood dwellers strengthen these very limits within which their territory is formally defined and protected. However, to confront the counter-operation of the residents, Minibar participants introduce instant solutions and continue performing their practice. Then, instead of pushing further, instead of offending the residents, the tactics of the participants include acting in agreeable ways to keep their place safe and to ease the discomfort of the residents to a point. Reciprocally, the residents sometimes show a degree of tolerance. As a result a balanced point is observed between the neighborhood residents and Minibar participants.

The tactics of Minibar participants are not developed deliberately, but spontaneously in response to the reactions of neighborhood residents. For instance, one of these tactics is an environmental concern and responsibility developed in response to the complaints of the residents. Many participant groups convey that they collect their trash before leaving and warn their friends to do so. Another one includes temporary recessions made to relax the residents and decrease the tension momentarily. When a warning comes or when the police patrols, Minibar crowds disperse or move to another street.

It should be strongly stressed that the spatial characteristics of Minibar constitute a complementary part of this tactical operation. The flexible spatiality of Minibar becomes a device in maintaining the continuation of Minibar. To summarize, the investigation of these rivalry relations reveals important issues. One is related to the tensions emerging within the act of creating Minibar. The act is not in conformity with every inhabitant's wishes; it transgresses the space of other inhabitants as it transgresses the established space; consequently it meets up with adverse reactions and interruptions. Nevertheless, the operation of the Minibar participants includes a struggle to maintain the endurance of the practice.

In conclusion, the investigation of these rivalry relations provides a picture of how re-defined spaces are created and sustained without being constructed and without aiming at any permanency. Minibar demonstrates that ephemerality and mobility allow the participants the possibility to endure their alternative practice, despite the existence of opposing and institutionalized parties and practices.

This is not the sole explanation for the continuation of Minibar in the district for a long period of time. The socio-economically high profile of the district and participants supports this. As the interviewees explain, Minibar participants are educated people coming from higher rank families. This influences the relationship in an encounter between the police and the participants; and verifies that Minibar is a safe place, providing freer conditions for socializing with respect to other leisure centers of Ankara.

Expressions and resistances in Minibar

A further intention of this study is to search for potential expressions and resistances in Minibar and to see whether the practice relates, for example, to a subculture-based identity,[8] to a political view, or to a lifestyle-based identity expression.[9] Yet none can be distinguished in Minibar. On the contrary, what had been observed among Minibar participants is the refusal of any affinity with such issues.

We rather observe that what constitutes Minibar is the leisure practice of a group of young people. It is not necessarily in response to social inequalities or class-based social polarizations; it does not aim to initiate social movements or the like. It is a daily act; it operates and it can be perceived only at that level of city life. There is no singular and definite consumption style, no dominant political view or opinion, but only an unorganized and un-institutionalized search for an ideal leisure practice. These expressions are also inherent in the preference for Minibar over established bars, comprising for instance, as summarized from the interviews, the possibility of being with friends and 'sharing', being able to benefit from the large and unlimited space of the street providing more freedom in bodily movements, being able to buy cheaper drinks or to mix your own drinks, as seen in Figure 5.8, not to be reckoned by your outlook, and so on. Thus, the expression of a demand for freer leisure practices.

Figure 5.8
Source: Can Altay, *Minibar Photograph Series*, 2002–2003.

To understand Minibar means, therefore, to uncover the needs, desires, and motives of Minibar participants. This is how, in the case of Minibar, the re-definition

---

8   See Hebdige, D. (1979), *Subculture: The Meaning of Style*.
9   Hetheringthon asserts the concept of 'expressive identities' in spite of lifestyle or subculture-based identity constructions. See Hetheringthon (1998).

of spaces provides a medium of expression. This will also help us understand what the practice of Minibar questions; hence we will explore the resistant meanings beyond Minibar.

Minibar had initially begun as part of the nightlife in Ankara; but from the beginning it was clear that it occupied a position that resisted it; because Minibar develops an alternative leisure activity, which refuses the expensive beverage prices and the established ways of functioning of the bars. Drinking on the streets, with friends and at cheaper prices is the common ground that brings Minibar participants together, as the participants express.

The comparison of Minibar with the established bars, as explained by the participants within their preference for Minibar, reveals the motives and demands behind the creation of Minibar. This comparison laid down the reasons why Minibar is preferred and frequented; and why Minibar came to compete with the existing nightlife of Ankara as an alternative leisure place. The new leisure practice introduced by Minibar challenges the existing nightlife norms; hence the practice of Minibar inheres a critical and resistant position against them in the way it re-formulates them.

The exploration of these resistant attitudes therefore indicates a search for idealized practices or conditions within the new uses or within the appropriated space. To conclude, it is possible to observe resistances in a re-defined space in two ways. The first is parallel to the transgression of the existing norms of urban space: it is the making of a space, a marginal space. The second runs beneath the transgressive operation of the groups of users, beneath what they express through their practices and acts. What they try to express, including what they express about themselves, may inform us about the culture and vision they share and also about what they try to emphasize, criticize, and about what they care for. Hence the resistance is not only opposing the existing order of urban space but also the established system the alternative practice connects to – nightlife.

So both the act of producing space and the created space itself provide a medium of expression and resistance for the alternative user group. Although implicit in Minibar, it can be explicit in other cases. The space of the inhabitants hence turns out to be a freer ground of expression and provides the possibility of countering the so-proclaimed death of the public sphere today.

Conclusion

The investigation of an actual and recent urban phenomenon such as Minibar, with the aim of uncovering hidden meanings, provides a view on a section of the city life, cutting through many different aspects of the spatial, social, cultural, economic, and political processes experienced by society.

Firstly, the close observation of the case of Minibar showed that the urban space could be manipulated, transformed, and (re)produced in the 'hands' of the inhabitants, after being produced and provided by the urban professionals and by the institutions or the investors. One of the main assertions in this article is that

Minibar can be accepted as the outcome of such an operation. This kind of creating space is formulated in this study as the re-definition of the urban space. This assertion is based on the works of Henri Lefebvre (1991) and Michel de Certeau (1984), and is exemplified in the investigation of Minibar. The elaboration of the issue through the case of Minibar provided the understanding that the urban space acquires new meanings and therefore a new definition through the development and practice of a new use in it. This particular 'way of using' includes, as postulated by de Certeau (1984), an act of production – the production of spaces. For instance, we have observed that the spaces of Minibar are produced by the practice of a newly introduced use, a leisure activity, that of socializing and drinking on the streets.

Secondly, the research implied that a new use is developed following the particular needs, demands, desires, and choices of the group who formulates and practices it. Accordingly, the practice of this new use carries particularities about the group. It is through the practice of this use that the group's members become represented in urban space and it is through this practice that the groups of inhabitants become able to express themselves, to manifest their attitudes and resistances, whether implicit or explicit. In association, it is seen that the spaces re-defined through the practice of these particular uses are the inventions of urban inhabitants in relation to circumstances weighing upon themselves.

Thirdly, it is under this pretext that Minibar participants justify their act because the introduced use and its implications on the existing urban space may not always be in conformity with the urban space itself and with the other users of the environment. In this respect, if the production of space by inhabitant groups is accepted as a search for another way, or as the outcome of a demand; another assertion can be made in relation to the research findings, suggesting that these spaces represent the sought-for solution, an idealized position that makes itself possible despite the existing, imposed conditions. Within this perspective the space of the inhabitants has a counter position and it intrinsically embeds a resistance.

Finally, creating urban space from a position of potential resistance is not so easily and smoothly accomplished. To maintain their space, the Minibar participants enter into a struggle and carry out a tactical operation. The spatiality, or in other words the spatial attributes, of the re-defined spaces (the ephemerality, the impermanency, the mobility, the flexibility) are the main assets of this operation. Other tactics are developed as spontaneous responses to the envisaged reactions. Yet it is only through this tactical operation that the inhabitants are able to create their spaces, to manifest their concerns and to exercise the practice they develop.

In conclusion, within this formulation, the lived space introduces itself as a medium of expression: an unlimited and un-intervened, free expression; not explicitly conveyed but hidden in the alternative practices of the inhabitant. Accordingly, the appropriated urban space proves to be an effective medium for acquiring knowledge of different inhabitant groups and for observing the influence of actual scenes on wider social, cultural, economic, and political processes.

References

Altaban, Ö. (1986), 'Ankara Kentsel Alanının Doğal Çevreye Yayılımı', in Tekeli *et al.* (eds).

Altay, C. (2003), *How Latitudes Become Forms: Art in a Global Age* catalogue text (Minneapolis: Walker Art Center).

Arksey, H. and Knight, P. (1999), *Interviewing for Social Scientists: An Introductory Resource with Examples* (London: Sage).

Bademli, R. (1986), 'Ankara Merkezi İş Alanının Gelişimi', in Tekeli *et al.* (eds).

Bauchard D.F. (ed.) (1977), *Language, Counter Memory Practice* (Oxford: Basil Blackwell).

Borden, I. (1998), 'Body Architecture', in Hill (ed.).

— (2001), 'Another Pavement, Another Beach: Skateboarding and the Performative Critique of Architecture', in Borden *et al.* (eds).

Borden *et al.* (eds) (2001), *The Unknown City: Contesting Architecture and Social Space* (London: Routledge).

Charmaz, K. (2003), 'Qualitative Interviewing and Grounded Theory Analysis', in Holstein and Gubrium (eds).

de Certeau, M. (1984), *The Practice of Everyday Life* (Berkeley: University of California Press).

Esterberg, K.G. (2002), *Qualitative Methods in Social Research* (USA: McGraw Hill).

Foucault, M. (1977), 'A Preface to Transgression', in Bauchard (ed.).

Gausa, M. (2003), 'Architecture Action', in Gausa *et al.* (eds).

Gausa *et al.* (eds) (2003), *The Metapolis Dictionary of Advanced Architecture: City, Technology and Society in the Information Age* (Barcelona: Actar).

Güvenç, M. (2001), 'Ankara'da Statü/Köken Farklılaşması; 1990 Sayım Örneklemleri Üzerinde "Blokmodel" Çözümlemeleri, in Yavuz (ed.).

Hebdige, D. (1979), *Subculture: The Meaning of Style* (London: Routledge).

Hetherington, K. (1998), *Expression of Identity: Space, Performance, Politics* (London: Routledge).

Hill, J. (1998), *Occupying Architecture: Between the Architect and the User* (London: Routledge).

Holstein, J.A. and Gubrium, J.F. (eds) (2003), *Inside Interviewing* (London: Sage).

Keith, M. and Pile, S. (eds) (1993), *Place and the Politics of Identity* (London, New York: Routledge).

Lefebvre, H. (1991), *The Production of Space* (Oxford: Blackwell).

Massey, D. (1993), 'Politics and Space/Time', in Keith and Pile (eds).

Morales, J. (2003), 'Infiltration', in Gausa *et al.* (eds).

Tekeli *et al.* (eds) (1986), *Ankara: 1985' ten 2015'e* (Ankara: EGO Genel Müdürlüğü).

Yavuz, Y. (ed.) (2001), *Tarih İçinde Ankara II* (Ankara: ODTÜ Mimarlık Fakültesi).

Internet-based references

Doron, G.M. (2000), *The Dead Zone & The Architecture of Transgression* <http://
www. geocities.com/gilmdoron/theDZ.html>, accessed March 2006.

Chapter 6

An Uncommon Common Space

Zeuler R.M.A. Lima and Vera M. Pallamin

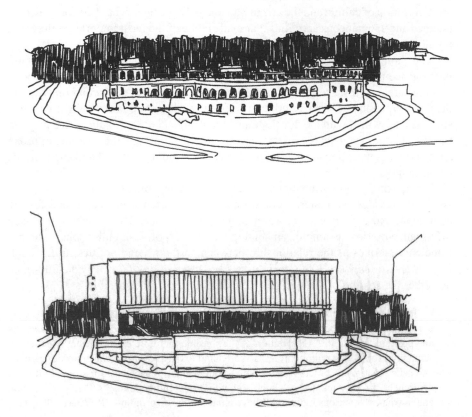

Figures 6.1 and 6.2 One space, two moments: Belvedere do Trianon and the Museum of Art of São Paulo (MASP) on Avenida Paulista

Source: Zeuler Lima.

Terraço do Trianon: Staging dissent and distribution

When architect Lina Bo Bardi designed the building for the Museum of Art of São Paulo (MASP) in the late 1950s in Brazil, she chose an uncommon configuration to occupy the space left by a traditional belvedere built in the 1910s. She replaced a solid building by a void space. As the opening illustrations show, she created a large glass container that seems to hover above a vast empty space called Terraço do Trianon [Trianon Terrace]. To her, this was no architectural extravaganza. The plaza was intended for the exercise of collective freedom. Her design transformed and enhanced the existing space as an urban viewing point – a threshold between city and architecture – and also as a stage for social practices. Because of the strategic position of the building in the city, the modernist practice of lifting the building from the ground opened up new possibilities for social manifestations. The terrace under the museum was initially conceptualized as part of a cosmopolitan project for the modernization of culture and the arts in São Paulo. Since then, it has been occupied by planned and spontaneous activities that made it one of the most important referential public spaces in the city.

The homogeneous appearance of the museum represents an important, heterogeneous symbolic place in São Paulo. Over almost fifty years, it has provided a unique arena and space for the encounter between cultural and social practices in the representation of collective urban life. The genealogy of this key collective urban space is intertwined with the development of Avenida Paulista [Paulista Avenue] and the city at large. Their shared history exemplifies how unstable the meaning of urban space is and how its transformation responds to conflicting cultural and social needs and meanings.

Terraço do Trianon offers both the actual and metaphorical features of theatrical space. It provides the material conditions for the presence of people and for the continuous expression, representation, and negotiation of collective acts. The terrace offers an empirical example, an analogy to what political philosopher Jacques Rancière describes as the relationship between aesthetics and politics. In his book *Le partage du sensible* (2000; in English *The Distribution of the Sensible* 2004), he describes the sharing of the symbolic, the distribution of the sensible, as

> […] the system of self-evident facts of sense perception that simultaneously discloses the existence of something in common and the delimitations that define the respective parts and positions within it. A distribution of the sensible therefore establishes at one and the same time something common that is shared and exclusive parts. This apportionment of parts and positions is based on a distribution of spaces, times, and forms of activity that determines the very manner in which something in common lends itself to participation and in what way various individuals have a part in this distribution. (Rancière 2004, 12)

The notion of the distribution of the sensible relates to Rancière's previous work *La mésentente*[1] (1995; English, *Disagreement* 1996), which proposes the notion of dissent as a counter-argument to liberal and Habermasian ideas of consensus. The notion of consensus defines political practice as the struggle between pre-defined voices or groups. Instead, according to Rancière, politics emerges out of the need of the excluded to affirm their presence and to have their identity recognized. This process ties political practice with symbolic representation. The convergence between aesthetics and politics provides an important insight into the fleeting meaning and social and physical constituency of urban spaces such as Terraço do Trianon. This approach to how aesthetics are politicized reveals how certain conditions of perception and expression are included or excluded in democratic cultural and social relations. Dissent is neither misunderstanding nor the unknown. Politics, in such terms, is the conflict around the existence of a common scene and those individuals and groups within it, and how those who do not have the right to be counted as 'speaking beings' achieve recognition and inclusion. Dissent is not a war of all against all, which would mean the absence of politics. Instead, it is the condition for the operation of political rationality (Rancière 1996).

Dissent relates emerging expressions with those that are already visible, pronounceable, or feasible in public spaces. It promotes ordered situations of conflict by creating new rules and new relationships, and encourages the inclusion of groups that have been either silenced or excluded from the constituency of the public sphere. Rancière is interested in how and by whom common spaces, discourses, and knowledge are produced, opened up, destabilized, and regulated. In other words, he analyzes the principles and rules that define the distribution of individual and collective roles and the forms of inclusion and exclusion within a certain community. These forms can be immaterial and material and, in our case, they include architectural and urban spaces. Rancière's approach to the distribution of the sensible and to dissent is grounded on the metaphor of staging. He suggests the political negotiation of collective and individual identities in the public sphere as the emergence of new visible, pronounceable or feasible actions and actors in public spaces.

The logic of dissent is the logic of otherness, and it translates the transformation of social subjects into political interlocutors. These emerging cultural and social voices constantly reinvent themselves at the same time that they reinvent the norms of the debate and the spaces of the city where such negotiations take place. Terraço do Trianon and MASP offer a good example of this logic. They are part of the contested history of inclusion and exclusion in the formal and informal production of urban space and in the public life of São Paulo. Since the creation of Avenida Paulista as a residential subdivision in 1891, the area currently occupied by the museum was reserved to be a collective urban space overlooking the city. The

---

1   Rancière proposes the term *mésentante* in French, which has been translated into English as 'disagreement'. However, we prefer the term 'dissent', which suggests a more uneasy meaning according to the Portuguese translation.

subdivision established a law prohibiting anything built on the site from obstructing this panorama. In 1911, the city built a large terraced structured on the site, which was demolished in 1951. The void space that exists today underneath MASP is both the windowsill and the image of collective urban life in the history of São Paulo. Its solemn emptiness has historically been interrupted many times by the vibrant presence of different social groups carrying their own forms of manifestation. As many of the illustrations in this article show, banners, posters, costumes, art works, temporary installations, flags, musical instruments, shields, and human barricades are just a few of the many tools used to accentuate the many voices and bodies to protest, celebrate and negotiate common values and social relationships. The collective appropriation of Terraço do Trianon shows how public administrations, civil society, and the citizenry have imagined, claimed, and occupied referential open spaces in the city as they have transformed their social and cultural relationships.

The creation and transformation of an urban common space

The origin of Terraço do Trianon is related to the development of Avenida Paulista as the most exclusive residential subdivision at the edges of the urban expansion of São Paulo in 1891. The city grew as a strategic urban center of the international coffee trade between the early 1870s and late 1920s, and Avenida Paulista became the home of the emerging economic elite. The original configuration of almost three kilometers of the avenue resembled residential European boulevards served by urban infrastructure that was uncommon to São Paulo at the time. The influence of French architecture was largely seen in the eclectic use of styles for the construction of private residences that progressively occupied the whole extension of the avenue.

The new subdivision occupied the crest of the hills that run from east to west and separate the two large valleys that configure the geography of São Paulo. In this strategic position, Avenida Paulista benefited from privileged views on the surrounding areas. One of these vistas was located one kilometer away from the western end of the Avenida Paulista, overlooking a valley and framing a wide perspective of the historic center. This place was reserved for a park officially opened in 1892 as Parque Villon [Villon Park], named after the French landscape architect who designed it. The park occupied both edges of the avenue: the south side incorporated an existing wooded area to house collective facilities, including a restaurant, and the north side remained unoccupied for a couple of decades. Park Villon was transformed into Terraço do Trianon in the 1910s. Mayor Raimundo Duprat bought the land and hired architect Ramos de Azevedo to design a terraced building overlooking the city center on the north side of the avenue. The terraces, finished in 1916 as shown in Figure 6.1, contained three pavilions and two pergolas on the upper level and a large luxury hall with restaurant and ballroom on the lower level. The south side was redesigned in 1918 by British landscape architect Barry Parker and officially named Parque do Trianon [Trianon Park].

These developments followed the urban transformations taking place in São Paulo since the 1870s, which radically transformed the image and the constituency of the city. The growth of the city and the accumulation of wealth in it were fostered by its strategic position between the areas of agricultural production in the hinterland of the state and the port of Santos. The city became the national leader in commercial and financial activities as well as in industrial production, and the population of São Paulo went from 20,000 to 600,000 inhabitants in fifty years (Sevcenko 2000, 78). Economic growth became more intense with the proclamation of the Brazilian Republic in 1889, which promoted a large influx of immigrants in both urban and rural areas. New urban residents constituted a massive working class and some of them eventually became merchants, professionals, investors, and industrialists. Urbanization expanded, but investments in infrastructure and public services were uneven, concentrating urban amenities in selected neighborhoods and starting the sharp spatial separation between wealthy and poor classes in the decades to come.

For almost twenty years, until the Great Depression affected the capitalist world, Parque do Trianon and the terraces were one of the main urban spaces staging the cultural, social, and political life of the agricultural, commercial, and industrial elites of São Paulo. They were the affluent space of social order and political consensus, or according to the terms suggested by Rancière, they represented the spaces of inclusion and exclusion that confirm the division of the community in social groups and positions. Among its frequent guests, there was a young group of artists and intellectuals gathered around the charismatic figure of writer and musician Mário de Andrade. Together they organized the 1922 Modern Art Week, which officially introduced modernism in Brazil.[2] This modernist group had an impressive pedigree. Some of the most influential artists and writers among them came from wealthy families and were in close contact with the early avant-garde movements taking place in Europe, particularly surrealism and futurism. They proposed that artists in Brazil should metaphorically devour the inflow of foreign cultural models, and produce a national version of digested modernism. Much of the work produced in this period had a nationalist drive and was expressive and critical of the local elite. Even though the main characters of the modernist movement were concerned with cultural democratization, their project did not embrace broad social, economic, or political reforms. The elitist origin of the movement did not address the disjunctions between the circulation of European modernizing projects and archaic political and social forms and popular cultural practices in the country.

In the meantime, there was another less lofty European influence leveraging political and social dissent in São Paulo, particularly through the massive immigration of Italian workers engaged in unions and anarchism. The nascent middle and working

---

2   The debate promoted by modernists about architecture in Brazil included issues about national identity, the renovation of formal and spatial languages based on technical transformations and building demands. Gregori Warchavichk designed two houses in São Paulo in the 1920s based on the architecture of Adolf Loos, which were responsible for the introduction of the principles of the modern movement in Brazil.

classes, including military officers, were growingly dissatisfied with the national political and economic life. In 1924, protest groups built barricades in strategic streets and public spaces in the historic center of the city and along Avenida Paulista in order to demonstrate against the rural and urban oligarchic groups that had tight control of the federal government. These protests gave visibility and voice to new political subjects in the modernization of São Paulo, destabilizing Avenida Paulista's affluent isolation. Federal troops contained the uprisings, and the local elites enjoyed a few more years of undisturbed prosperity, represented by the slogan 'São Paulo, the Fastest Growing City' in Brazil. However, the financial crisis in the New York Stock Exchange in 1929 profoundly affected the trade and the monoculture of coffee in the country and led many producers and traders to declare bankruptcy, generating widespread unemployment. This event changed the social and political structure of the country and the city, creating opportunities for new leading groups, and later the emergence of a sizeable urban middle class. Many of the families who resided along Avenida Paulista lost their fortunes and had to sell their properties to an emerging elite of merchants and small industrialists that grew in the shadow of the coffee economy.

In the beginning of the 1930s, the avenue became the stage for political demonstrations, which led to the Constitutional Revolution of 1932. This time the dissent was in the hands of the local emerging elites, who fought to regain control of the national political scene. Demonstrations opposed the regime that made Getúlio Vargas president after a coup against the election of Julio Prestes in 1930. They demanded the return of the political autonomy of state governments and the separation of the state of São Paulo from the Brazilian federation. These conflicts lasted three months, until federal troops controlled them.

During Getúlio Vargas' regime, between 1930 and 1945, São Paulo consolidated its economic and industrial leadership in Brazil under a centralized technocratic state. The policies established after the collapse of the coffee economy were particularly beneficial to the industrialization of São Paulo and the concentration of wealth and new urban development around Avenida Paulista. This period saw intense urban development in São Paulo and transformation of the role of Avenida Paulista as a public space. Two important complementary processes linking urban planning ideas and real estate development affected Avenida Paulista. Zoning and building laws were proposed for the city. Mayor Prestes Maia devised a master plan for São Paulo named *Plano de Avenidas* (Plan of Avenues) in 1930 based on Burnham's plan for Chicago in order to promote controlled urban growth. For years, Prestes Maia argued that previous public administrations had privileged infrastructural investments since World War I, without defining comprehensive principles for the organization of a fast-growing metropolis. He insisted that the city invest in visionary urban planning.

Maia's master plan incorporated Avenida Paulista as a main artery connected by a series of avenues departing from the historic center of the city. This was the first (and also the last) time that morphology and aesthetics were part of a comprehensive reflection about the urban design and development of the city of

São Paulo. His goal was to promote urban decentralization, low-cost and high-density housing, and automobile circulation. Prestes Maia was appointed mayor in 1938, during Vargas' first mandate. Maia gradually implemented modified parts of his plan, by promoting the construction of high-rise buildings based on setback and Floor Area Ratio (FAR) legislation, and creating mortgage policies. Maia's mandate ended in 1945 and his Plan of Avenues never achieved full completion. As a result, the city was left with a deficient regulatory system of streets and infrastructure, and lack of new open public spaces. With urban development in the hand of real estate interests, public squares, parks, and plazas became scarcer as the city grew. By privileging the circulation of cars over pedestrians and public transport, the city initiated a long process of technocratic planning, with little room to consider public spaces as places for the enhancement of collective ordinary public life.

The imbalance between aggressive speculative activities by the real estate market, the limitation of Prestes Maia's plan, and the absence of subsequent regulatory plans altogether produced a new pattern in the city defined as *verticalização* (vertical growth), which is best exemplified by the boom of high-rise construction in São Paulo from the 1940s to the 1960s (Somekh 1997). Avenida Paulista followed this process. Developers pressured legislators to change zoning and building regulations in order to demolish existing villas and to build residential and commercial high-rises. In 1936, the city government had already approved legislation allowing commercial activities and the construction of residential buildings on Avenida Paulista for the first time. Typological changes came together with density changes, and massive buildings replaced the gaps left by large domestic gardens. These changes largely attracted the middle class to the area in the early 1950s as well as affected the uses and the purpose of Terraço do Trianon as a space of reference in the city. Following the accentuation of vertical growth in the post-war period and the creation of new urban regulations, Avenida Paulista attracted new residents and traditional commercial and financial activities previously located in the historic downtown.

The years between 1945 and 1964 represented an important period of democratization and industrialization in Brazil. The restructuring of capitalism after World War II together with the consolidation or architectural modernism in Brazil and president Juscelino Kubitschek's nation-building project changed the economic and urban dynamics of the nation and of São Paulo. Kubitschek aspired to modernize Brazil in a very short period during his mandate from 1950 to1955. His plan, which followed the slogan '50 years in 5 years', culminated with the construction of Brasilia as the new federal capital. São Paulo largely benefited from this plan both in terms of urban and economic growth and in social and cultural transformation. Its development also attracted massive migration from poorer areas of the country, which intensified the appearance of shantytowns. Once again, the population of São Paulo boomed – from 2.6 million in 1950 to 4.7 million in 1960 (Sevcenko 2000, 78) – reinforcing the spatial division between the affluent center and poor peripheries and also expanding the cultural repertoires as well as the social problems of the city. Avenida Paulista became the favored place for the installation of national and multinational companies and banks in the city in the early 1950s, while industrial production grew in the western municipalities of the metropolitan region.

The old structure of Terraço do Trianon did not survive the changes along Avenida Paulista. The park started to lose its selective users as the fashionable ballroom was more and more used for bolero and samba gatherings promoted by a nascent mass-cultural industry. This scenario differed from the lofty modernist aspirations that accompanied the increasing market value of land along Avenida Paulista. Consequently, mayor Adhemar de Barros ordered the demolition of the whole ensemble in 1951. Later that same year, the lot returned to the control of Paulistano elites as Ciccillo Mattarazzo, heir of one of the most affluent industrialists in the city, sponsored the construction of temporary pavilions for the first International Art Biennial in São Paulo.[3] After the end of the exhibition, the site remained empty. The city administration tried to develop the area as a cultural center but the legal determination to maintain the view open towards the city limited architectural proposals for the area.

The hiatus during which the lot remained empty marked the beginning of strong transformations in the urban structure and in the social, and cultural practices along Avenida Paulista. In the late 1950s, Assis Chateaubriand and Pietro Maria Bardi – architect Lina Bo Bardi's husband – the directors of the Museum of Art of São Paulo, and Lina herself saw a unique opportunity to use the lot. They successfully negotiated the relocation of the museum, created in 1947, from its temporary facilities in the historic downtown to a permanent address on Avenida Paulista. Lina Bo Bardi proposed an architectural solution that respected the existing legislation, including keeping the terrace unobstructed. The museum design separated the building into two parts: a semi-buried block containing auditoria, library, exhibition halls and a restaurant topped by the terrace, and a transparent building for exhibitions and the permanent collection above, hanging from two long piers spanning almost 240 feet. Lina Bo Bardi's proposal preserved and re-conceptualized the historic space of Terraço do Trianon as a permanent open space to be formally used by the museum and also informally appropriated by the population of São Paulo. In one of her watercolors, she imagined the terrace being used for activities from art exhibitions to a large, colorful playground.

MASP, Avenida Paulista and the reconfiguration of Terraço do Trianon

Lina Bo Bardi conceived the museum in the late 1950s, a time of great cultural and economic enthusiasm in Brazil in general and in São Paulo in particular. The 1950s marked the high point of emergence and expansion of the representative functions

---

3   The first Ciccillo Mattarazzo, the heir of a large industrial fortune, created the International Art Biennial of São Paulo. He also created the Museum of Modern Art in 1949 in order to compete with Assis Chateaubriand's Museum of Art of São Paulo.

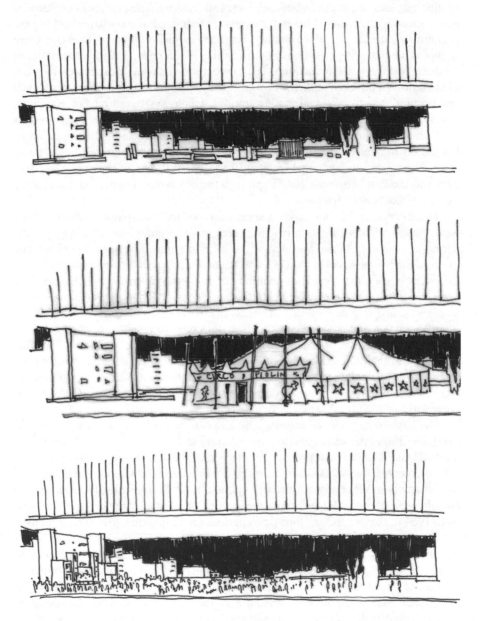

Figures 6.3 to 6.5 The staging of different public uses as imagined and promoted by Lina Bo Bardi on Terraço do Trianon: art exhibitions, circus installation, and music shows
Source: Zeuler Lima.

of the State initiated at the end of the nineteenth century. The previous two decades had intensified the national bases for capitalist industrial accumulation and for the economic modernization of the country. From the cultural point of view, architecture occupied a unique, important position. Brazilian modernism expanded the limits of aesthetic invention and production. The emergence of strong local expressions out of the inflow of different influences contributed to the renovation of the international architectural debate. National modernization, which was based on fast economic development, found fertile symbolic ground in São Paulo. The city celebrated its 400th anniversary in 1954 with several cultural projects, including the creation of Parque do Ibirabuera, designed by the team of collaborators headed by architect Oscar Niemeyer and landscape architect Roberto Burle-Marx. The ample, modern park was the first large-scale public space in the city whose population had already exceeded 2,000,000 inhabitants.

These events and the initiatives and expectations for the expansion of democratic participation and civil rights provided a progressive context for the design of the permanent building of the Museum of Art of São Paulo. The spatial performance of the museum on Avenida Paulista was based on an aesthetic and political thesis that went beyond the ingenuous solution for the legal constraints of the site. The new building created an unforeseen staging in the city. Its architectural scale, ampleness, and free accessibility announced Lina Bo Bardi's concern with spaces of emancipation and political equality. Her design is the result of aesthetic choices that favor, in the light of Rancière's suggestions, equality and inclusion. Equality, according to the philosopher, is not a goal but a principle, the ground for all the regimes of distribution of the sensible. Democratic emancipation is an intermittent process that takes place through disturbances in the established system of social inequalities.

The large, empty terrace imagined by Lina Bo Bardi literally opened room for everyday life: to performances, to tensions, and to contradictions which over time have defined its referential presence in the life of the city as illustrated by Figures 6.3, 6.4, and 6.5. Ten years passed between the initial conception of the museum and its construction. When it was officially opened in 1968, ironically, the country had already been living under the repressive forces of a military dictatorship that lasted from 1964 to the late 1980s. During this period, the centralized government focused investments in the development of large-scale urban infrastructure and in state-controlled heavy industry. It also reinforced the opening of Brazilian economy to multinational corporations and financial institutions. At the same time, governmental support of social welfare and cultural programs for a booming urban population decreased substantially by comparison. São Paulo concentrated the formation of large oligopolies that controlled the national economy in the following decades.

Avenida Paulista benefited largely from the economic boom of the early 1970s and started to look like North American Central Business Districts (CBDs) as corporate high-rises reshaped its skyline. It became the main artery in the transportation system of the city, connecting several prosperous areas of São Paulo. Meanwhile, at the street level, the oppressive nature of the military regime limited the collective and public life of Brazilian citizens, creating a visible impact on the use of urban open spaces. Dissent was outlawed. A large contingent of the population did not have access to the rights of citizenship. The impoverishment of rural populations accentuated migration flows towards major metropolitan areas such as São Paulo, which had no systematic plan for the provision of jobs and housing to accommodate the booming urban population. The city concentrated investments in the remodeling and expansion of infrastructure and public services in consolidated urban areas, while growing and impoverished peripheries remained underserved by public efforts of modernization. Shantytowns and tenements quickly expanded, reinforcing the spatial, social, and political differences in São Paulo.

Figure 6.6   Terraço do Trianon and MASP emerge as a referential place for the collective manifestation of dissent in São Paulo
Source: Zeuler Lima.

However, the pervasive climate of economic depression that followed the oil crisis of 1973 and political oppression stimulated unions, left-wing intellectuals, and the progressive wing of the Catholic Church to organize strikes and resistance against the military regime. They had great impact in the course of the authoritarian regime and strengthened union movements, which organized several strikes in São Paulo between 1978 and 1979. These strikes mobilized millions of workers locally and nationally in demonstrations in urban open spaces such as Avenida Paulista and through telecommunication media as showed in Figure 6.6.

Throughout this process, the Museum of Art of São Paulo maintained its important position in the cultural life of the city, both externally and internally. Lina Bo Bardi organized a large exhibition in the museum in 1969 titled *The Hands of the Brazilian People*, in which she exhibited objects produced by people mostly in the poorest areas in the north and northeast of the country. She described such expressions of popular art and everyday life as the result of the struggle for survival under very adverse economic and environmental conditions. The exhibition was a veiled protest against the discriminatory cultural projects of Brazil's ruling classes. In another provoking gesture, she had *Circo Piolin* [Piolin Circus] installed under the museum, honoring the popular actor and clown whose work had great influence in the Modern Art Week in the 1920s as seen in Figure 6.5. As a result of her cultural provocations and increased participation in underground politics, Lina Bo Bardi had to leave the country for a few periods of exile in the 1970s.

**Figure 6.7   Public demonstrations find place under and
              around the Museum of Art of São Paulo**
Source: Zeuler Lima.

The gradual demise of the military regime in Brazil in the 1980s left a profound economic and social crisis behind. In 1984, several demonstrations of a widespread movement opposing the dictatorship called *Diretas Já* [Elections Now] gathered 1.3

million people and took place in several areas of the city, along Avenida Paulista, and at Terraço do Trianon. This movement contributed to the gradual transition of the military regime into the reconstruction of democratic life in Brazil. Since then, MASP has become one of the main stages of dissent and emergence of new political voices and subjects in the public life of the city. The most important among such events was the *Caras-Pintadas* [Painted Faces] movement in 1992, enacted by a massive and noisy crowd in support of the impeachment of president Collor de Mello who had ironically been elected president for the first time in 1989 since the end of the dictatorship. The museum and the terrace gained great notoriety and the population of São Paulo started to use the plaza as a departure point for social and political demonstrations illustrated in Figure 6.7.

The public enthusiasm of the late 1980s and early 1990s introduced new subjects and groups in the political scene of the country. Old groups repositioned themselves as new constituencies appeared in the national scene. One of the novelties was the ascendance of the left-wing Partido dos Trabalhadores [Workers' Party]. The party came out of steel-mill union movements – under the leadership of Luis Inácio Lula da Silva, who was elected as president in 2002 – and from different sectors of the left in the country, which included intellectuals, part of the Church and people who had received amnesty from the military regime as demonstrated in Figure 6.6. Under Fernando Henrique Cardoso's presidency during the 1990s, the country adopted neo-liberal policies dictated by global capitalism. Despite the stabilization of currency, urban social problems aggravated. By that time, the constructive potential of Avenida Paulista had reached the maximum legal construction ratio, and real estate investments moved to other parts of the city, causing economic decline in the area. This change made the pedestrian spaces of the avenue more porous to the social diversity and public manifestations in the city: from soccer celebrations to political demonstrations, from antique fairs to areas of male prostitution, from street vendors and business to homeless people. In response to undesired forms of spatial appropriation of the avenue, property owners along Avenida Paulista have lobbied in the city administration for projects of urban revitalization that are highly defensive and privatizing. Surveillance systems with cameras and private security guards have increasingly taken over the control of public spaces. The avenue, which was the symbol of urban and cultural life between the 1960s and 1980s, has surrendered to the image of a highly controlled and privatized domain.

As part of this scenario, significant transformations have occurred in the relationship between the Museum of Art of São Paulo and the city since the late 1990s. Pietro Maria Bardi resigned as the director of the museum in 1990, and the board of trustees replaced him with developer and architect Júlio Neves in 1995. Neves proposed drastic changes to the original mission and architectural layout of the museum, including restrictions to the use of Terraço do Trianon. At the end of 2005, he presented a proposal to buy the property east of the museum in order to build a 120 meter high tower. The new building should allow a panoramic view of the whole city and would also place the Museum at its feet. The purpose of this astounding development was to promote tourism and to generate income for the institution. The proposal generated great controversy and, after widespread debate in the press and in professional circles, the project was vetoed by Compresp, the Municipal Council for Preservation of Historic, Cultural and Environmental Heritage of the City of São Paulo. The decision was based on the argument that the Museum occupies an important referential place in the urban landscape and that surrounding new buildings should be limited to a lower height.

Budget problems, the concern with safety, the increasing commodification of art and culture, and the growth of tourist industry have made the museum less accessible in the last decade. After decades of free access and public support, the museum

Figure 6.8 Public celebrations under and around the Museum of Art of São Paulo
Source: Zeuler Lima.

started to charge admission fees and to raise funds from corporations in order to promote its activities. It also had to take care of the physical deterioration of the concrete structure and mechanical systems, which were restored by the new administration. The risk of overload on the concrete structure that sustains the terrace led the museum to prohibit its use by large audiences, coinciding with the desire for legal control of mass cultural and political events on Avenida Paulista as envisioned by representatives of business and financial institutions located on the avenue. MASP also lost its unique prominence in the city's cultural circle, since it has become part of a wider group of private and public museums and cultural institutions, many of them located along the area of Avenida Paulista.

Despite these problems, Terraço do Trianon has not lost its referential presence in the social imaginary of São Paulo and in the physical space of Avenida Paulista. On the contrary, the convergence between MASP and the avenue still enjoys a privileged position. There is nothing like it in the whole metropolis. The strategic location of the museum continues to provide public visibility, and recent restrictions have altered but not stopped the collective appropriation of this important place and landmark. After almost forty years, the conversion between Avenida Paulista and Terraço do Trianon continue to be the primary urban reference for different social groups in their practice of cultural and political dissent. These manifestations cover a wide spectrum as exemplified in Figure 6.8: protests, strikes, demonstrations for social recognition such as the annual gay pride parade, artistic performances, and collective celebrations such as soccer championships, to mention just a few.

Final considerations

Terraço do Trianon, the large open space under the concrete span of the Museum of Art of São Paulo (MASP), has served as an important stage for the negotiation of social and cultural values in the history of the city since the beginning of the twentieth century. The genealogy of the meaning of this open urban space is intertwined with struggles for material and symbolic representation in the city. These conflicts have interplayed with the development of the city, the growth of its population, and the changing values that are associated to this process. The notion of dissent and the distribution of the sensible proposed by Jacques Rancière are important recourses for expanding the understanding history, public spaces, public culture, democracy, and citizenship as shared and disputed dimensions of urban life. As we saw in regard to Avenida Paulista in general and to MASP in particular, the emergence of new voices in the political arena changes the appropriation of urban open spaces. New meanings are attributed to such spaces according to the relationship of otherness that takes place in them. The public sphere provides situations for the encounter and conflict between the logic of maintenance of social order and status quo and the logic of dissent, which transforms the border between public and private and amplifies the representation of those who count publicly. The expansion of actual, material, and symbolic representation; moral recognition of citizens; and the effort for the democratization of social relations involve, as shown in this article, political struggles that have wide cultural significance, which often imply the advance and the retreat of a whole nation.

The open space Lina Bo Bardi incorporated in her proposal for the Museum of Art of São Paulo (1967) is a unique example of how designers imagine and represent collective spaces, and how they are socially appropriated, confirmed, or rejected by different social groups. Despite the museum's vulnerability to historic changes, the current uses and appropriation of the areas around it still fulfill Lina Bo Bardi's aspiration for Terraço do Trianon as a space for the exercise of free thought and spontaneous social practices. She liked to say that critics did not like her design for the museum but insisted that people in general did, sardonically adding: 'Do you know who did this? It was a woman!'

References

Andrade, C.R.M. (1998), *Barry Parker – Um arquiteto inglês na cidade de São Paulo* (São Paulo: FAUUSP, Tese de Doutorado).

Bardi, L.B. (1967), 'O novo Trianon 1957–1967' in *O Mirante das Artes* September/ October, no. 5 (São Paulo).

Maia, F.P. (1930), *Introdução ao estudo de um plano de avenidas para a cidade de São Paulo* (São Paulo: Melhoramentos).

MASP – Assis Chateaubriand Ano 30 (1978) (São Paulo: Secretaria da Cultura, Ciência e Tecnologia do Governo do Estado de São Paulo).

Rancière, J. (1995), *La Mésentente – Politique et Philosophie* (Paris: Galilée).

Rancière, J. (1996), *O Desentendimento* (São Paulo: Editora 34).

Rancière, J. (1999), *Disagreement – Politics and Philosophy* (Minneapolis: University of Minnesota Press).

Rancière, J. (2000), *Le partage du sensible – Esthétique et Politique* (Paris: La Fabrique).

Rancière, J. (2004), *The Politics of Aesthetics: The Distribution of the Sensible* (New York: Continuum).

Sevcenko, N. (2000), *Pindorama Revisitada* (São Paulo: Fundação Peirópolis).

Somekh, N. (1997), *A cidade vertical e o urbanismo modernizador* (São Paulo: Edusp).

Chapter 7

Seeing Succession in Little and Big Italy – Encountering Ethnic Vernacular Landscapes

Jerome Krase

Introduction

There are many ways that individuals and groups encounter each other in urban spaces. The most frequently cited occasions are direct, face to face social interactions, but communciation and social exchange also takes place via the physical, visible environment. For example, when people walk down a city street they are exposed to a myriad of images which give them clues to who may or may not dominate in the neighborhood. This illustrated essay on urban neighborhoods in the United States and Italy is the latest in a long series based on research which I have conducted about how the meanings of neighborhood spaces are changed by the agency of even the least of their inhabitants (Krase 2002). It attempts to demonstrate how Italian American neighborhoods in United States, specifically New York City, are similar to Italian neighborhoods in Italy, specifically Rome, in the way that they have been changed by the invasion of new and different ethnic groups. The spatial and semiotic logic of diasporic/transnational processes is presented here in the form of images; especially of encounters between ethnic groups as represented in changing commercial vernacular landscapes. In the Italian American case this process of what the classic urban ecologists called 'ethnic succession' is analogous to the aphorism of fish swallowing other fish. For more than a century Italian immigrants to the United States have been changing the meanings of central city spaces. Most stereotypically they created Italian Colonies and Little Italies in one form or another. They accomplished this not merely by the power of superior numbers of local inhabitants but by the momentum of spatial semiotics, i.e. changing the appearances of spaces and places and thereby changing their meanings as well. By the 1970s the demography as well as the meanings of many of those Italian American ethnicized spaces was being challenged by the influx of new groups. Today some of the best known of these Little Italies remain as little more than what I have called 'Italian American Ethnic Theme Parks', places which are virtually Italian in name only.

Back in the country of origin, although Italy has for centuries been a major source of emigrants it has only been since the 1980s that it has been the recipient of large numbers of foreigners seeking more than temporary residence. Even more recently, the demography of quintessentially Italian cities has been changing in response to immigrants. As we can consider how American urban spaces became Italianized and subsequently became less so, we should be able to consider how Italian spaces lose their own, indigenous *Italianità* in response to immigrant settlements and local commercial practices.

In order to demonstrate how Italian central cities have become as American ones cities, an idea once rejected as almost absurd, both old and new approaches are needed. The old is represented by Robert Ezra Park and Ernest Burgess' classical ecological theory of invasion and succession of urban neighborhoods. The new is represented theoretically by spatial semiotics and methodologically by visual sociology. After briefly discussing these theories and methods we will turn to a consideration of the changing meanings, illustrated by select images, of ethnically contested spaces in New York City and Rome. The New York City selections are from my recent studies of historical Little Italies (Krase 1999), and in Central Rome, of the changing Esquilino neighborhood. The Esquilino is one of the areas that I observed and photographed while at the University of Rome in 1998 to study 'New Immigrants to Rome'. I returned in 2003 and re-photographed most of the same streetscapes. Here I will focus on the commercial landscape, store windows and shop signs which are interpreted by ordinary people as ethnic markers. It is interesting to note that the strongest semiotic parallel exists with the invasion of both these Little and Big Italy neighborhoods by Asians, especially Chinese. There is also a great irony in these parallels in that during the period of mass migration Americans saw Italians as an integral part of an invading unwashed horde as do contemporary Italians visualize a much smaller influx of documented and undocumented Asian and other aliens.

Italianità

Mine is not the only work that emphasizes the importance of understanding the essential semiotic/symbolic character of *Italianità*. Italian Americanist Fred L. Gardaphe refers to signs indicating qualities such as *omerta* and *bella figura* (1996, 20). My own work identified the spatial and visible components of the complex, as yet undeconstructed, notion of *Italianità* such as how notions of both *omerta* and *bella figura* are visually available as social performance and in vernacular architecture (Krase 1993). As Mike Davis argued for *Latinidad* I would submit that *Italianità* 'is *practice* rather than representation' (2001, 15). In a related vein, Roland Barthes once wrote that he had watched on television what he thought was 'a very French film' 'Why very French?' he asked.

> We see a young woman take her dresses out of the closet and stuff them in her suitcase: she is leaving the conjugal bed and board – situation, adultery, crisis. Well, then it is a

good dramatic film. Here is what makes it French: the actors seem to spend their time in a café or at family meals. Here the strange stereotype is nationalized: it belongs to the setting, not to history: hence it has a meaning, not a function. (1985, 103)

It is agency which transforms mere representation into practice. I use a simple formula for this process; members of ethnic groups by going about their daily existence present themselves; the observer re-presents their performances in description; which in turn becomes a representation. Roland Barthes and Mike Davis clearly indicate the necessity of exploring the role played by space and place in ethnicity and ethnic identity of all self or otherwise identified social groups. It might be useful for us to think for a moment of immigrant neighborhoods as 'Third Spaces' or interstitial places where things such as ethnic identity are being created and then negotiated, demonstrating in this way the agency of ordinary people (Gutiérrez 1999). Whereas much of Third Space discourse concerns the negotiation of identities of persons within real and imagined spaces, my own special interest is on how those identities change the meaning of the space in which ethnicity is acted out or practiced. Consequently one can also consider how the newly defined space affects the identities of the people within it. I would argue that by doing *Italianità*, Italian immigrants to America socially created Little Italics. In the same way then, we can argue that new immigrants by displaying their own cultural and social practices are undoing *Italianità* in both Little Italy and, for want of a better euphemism, 'Big Italy'.

Ethnic succession

University of Chicago sociologists Robert Park and Ernest Burgess developed an elaborate notion, more of a general descriptive formula than a theory, of city growth and development (1925). It supposes that cities were like natural environments and as such were influenced by forces that also affected natural ecosystems. The most important of these forces was competition, which was expressed in the struggle for scarce resources such as living space and jobs. They argued that competition resulted in 'natural areas' dominated by people with shared social and economic characteristics. City-wide competition for the most desirable residential or commercial spaces would be expressed in the form of concentric zones. Their model was not static, and movement from one zone to the other was termed 'succession'. For our purposes here this logic was demonstrated by less able migrants strangely 'dominating' the least desirable residential sections in urban centers. The classic pattern in American central cities during periods of high immigration had been the development of immigrant enclaves in 'zones of transition' such as Little Sicily and Chinatown in Chicago located near the central business districts. Rome's zone of transition might well be found around the central station in the Esquilino. With few other exceptions, the oldest of Rome's central areas have been the most protected from radical change. In recent decades much has subtly changed, and today even working-class run-down areas are being gentrified. Since the 1990s what were the least desirable areas for residence and commerce, near the central station, have also been 'in transition'.

Ethnic succession results from the competition between new and established groups and is often facilitated by the out-migration of the more advantaged group. Compared to the United States, residential mobility in Italy is slow. Therefore opportunities for housing are limited. In contrast to places like New York City, for example, most Roman neighborhoods are not transformed in a matter of a decade. This history-in-the-making can nevertheless be easily compared to the centuries-old processes of invasion and succession that have characterized major cities in the United States. Cities like New York have long been the destination of immigrants and ecologically understandable spatial patterns had already been established. Large-scale immigration, legal and otherwise, is relatively new to Italy, where an interest in American urban sociology has been increasing in recent decades. With few exceptions, most European sociologists thought of American cities as of a different species from their own. My work points to greater similarities than previously assumed. In much the same way that the appearance of Italian American central city neighborhoods has changed in response to late 20th century documented and undocumented immigration, so are Italy's vernacular urban landscapes changing today.

Spatial semiotics and visual sociology

The question for pre- and post-modern urbanologists has not been 'Who or what is where in the city?' but 'how and why' they got there. Researchers look at the same objects but the meanings of those objects seem to vary by the ideology of the viewer. The purely descriptive models of classical urban ecology come from a biological analogy. In the city, equilibrium is expressed through the interaction of human nature with geographical and spatial factors producing 'natural' areas. Political economists, on the contrary, see these natural areas and ecological zones as the result of 'uneven development', and perhaps even planned cycles of decay and renewal. Globalization and the movement of labor have changed the meaning of spaces in both Italian America and in Italy.

The landscapes of both Italian America and Italy are affected by 'natural' and migration-driven demographic forces, as well as the powerful processes of globalization, de-industrialization, and privatization. As I have argued elsewhere,

> [...] contemporary urban sociologists appear to be suffering from parallax vision. One eye sees the 'natural' spatial form and function of the city as a biological analogy as did Parks and Burgess. The other eye sees these same urban places and spaces as the reproductions of power, and circuits of capital. a la Castells (1989), Harvey (1989), and Lefebvre (1991). (Krase 2004, 17)

I must emphasize that my research into ethnicity and space has not been merely a theoretical exercise. It has important practical applications to the present and future problems of Italian cities, which are unprepared to deal with the rapidity of ethnic and racial change engendered by globalization and the development of a European Union.

For most, a visual approach in the humanities and social sciences is taking or showing pictures as an adjunct to the 'regular' process of research. Visual sociology is much more than that. In my own work it is both a theoretical and methodological practice for 'producing and decoding images which can be used to empirically investigate social organization, cultural meaning and psychological processes' (Grady 1996, 14). I focus upon what John Brinkerhoff Jackson calls 'vernacular landscapes', which are part of the life of communities, and which are governed by custom and held together by personal relationship (1984, 6). Italian administrators and planners of multiethnic cities could benefit greatly from an understanding of immigrant and ethnic vernacular urban landscapes, which is according to Dolores Hayden, 'an account of both inclusion and exclusion' (1991, 7).

In a related vein, Harvey argued that:

> Different classes construct their sense of territory and community in radically different ways. This elemental fact is often overlooked by those theorists who presume a priori that there is some ideal-typical and universal tendency for all human beings to construct a human community of roughly similar sort, no matter what the political or economic circumstances. (1989, 265)

Visual sociology and vernacular landscapes are connected via spatial semiotics. Mark Gottdiener writes that 'the study of culture which links symbols to objects is called semeiotics' and 'spatial semeiotics studies the metropolis as a meaningful environment' (1994, 15–16). 'Seeing' the uses and/or meanings of space requires sensitivity and understanding of the particular culture that creates, maintains, and uses the re-signified space. In other words even the most powerless of urban dwellers is a social 'agent' and therefore participates in the local reproduction of regional, national, and global societal relations.

According to Gottdiener (1994) the most basic concept for urban studies study is the 'settlement space', which is both constructed and organized.

> It is built by people who have followed some meaningful plan for the purposes of containing economic, political, and cultural activities. Within it people organize their daily actions according to meaningful aspects of the constructed space. (1994, 16)

As part of national and global systems, neighborhoods are affected by a wide range of supply-side forces. The connection made between Italian and Italian American vernacular landscape shows that ordinary people can affect their environment, even though they are ultimately at the mercy of larger societal forces. Visual sociology and attention to vernacular landscapes in the inner city allows us to see conflict, competition, and dominance at a level noticed only by local residents.

New York City's Little Italies

In *White Ethnic Neighborhoods and Assimilation* Alba, Crowder, and Logan looked at white ethnic neighborhoods to see the degree of assimilation of Germans, Irish, and Italians in the Greater New York region in 1980 and 1990 (1997). Italians, they found, still had many and large neighborhoods. However, from the 1980s, most of those located in central cities were declining due to the invasion and succession of minorities in inner-city neighborhoods by minorities. Most of these newcomers were new, non-European immigrant groups for whom the doors were opened wider by the 1965 and subsequent immigration laws. In addition to these regularized groups was a large influx of undocumented aliens. Racial incidents such as those in Italian American Bensonhurst reminded the authors that Italian Americans vigorously defend their turf, even though at the same time Manhattan's famous Little Italy became home to primarily Chinese. I note here that in the first decade of the 21st century Brooklyn's Bensonhurst area is being transformed by the influx of Chinese, other Asians, as well as Russian immigrants. Bensonhurst's major commercial street, 18th Avenue, still carries the title Cristoforo Columbo Boulevard. In The Bronx, Belmont is home to many Albanians and Latinos. In all cases, these areas are still referred to as 'Little Italies'.

Little Italy is a product and source of both social and cultural capital. Although ordinary people in the neighborhood are ultimately at the mercy of distant structural forces, in their naiveté they continue to create and modify the local spaces allocated to them, and inevitably become part of the urban landscape. Thusly people and spaces become symbols and as a result, they come to merely represent themselves and thereby lose their autonomy. The enclave comes to symbolize its imagined inhabitants and stands for them independent of their residence in it. Localized reproductions of cultural spaces can also be easily commodified and presented as spectacle for visitors such as tourists.

No model or stereotype can ever adequately represent the multiple realities of Italian, or any other, ethnic-America. There is too much in the way of permutations of generations, continuity, and change. But for many novelists, script writers, as well as social scientists, Little Italy represents the idea of Italian America. I have suggested that idealized ethnic urban spaces, both 'representations of spaces' as well as 'spaces of representation', can be summarized as follows: oblivion, ruination, ethnic theme parks, immigration museums, and anthropological gardens.

1. Oblivion means 'the state of being forgotten' and here we find ethnic enclaves

erased by urban renewal, highways, bridges, and other construction.

2. Ruins are the rubble of neighborhoods often abandoned in anticipation of 'renewal', or cleared of misnamed 'slums', which await new uses. These 'liminal' zones of 'in-betweenness' are on their way toward oblivion.

3. Ethnic theme parks, such as Little Italies, are preserved as spectacles for the appreciation of tourists (Krase 1997).

The primary focus in this paper are Little Italies and Italian cities as theme parks, or spectacles for tourists. What they have in common is that they are visible commodified cultural representations. David Harvey explains that the 'organization of spectacles' can be part of 'the production of an urban image' which is an 'important facet of interurban competition' as 'urban strategies to capture consumer dollars' (1989, 233). Although he is primarily concerned with the modern or post modern version of 'display of the commodity' (271), under the constraints of 'flexible accumulation' he notes that since the ancient Roman 'bread and festivals' spectacles have existed as a means of social control (270). In short, the creation and maintenance of spectacle is associated with a highly fragile patterning of urban investment as well as increasing social and spatial polarization of urban class antagonisms (273).

One ought to think of the photographs as text about the contested meanings of Italianness; a visual symbolic competition which reflects the battle for the dominance of the spaces themselves. Wei's obviously Chinese Gift Shop is in Bensonhurst, Brooklyn's fading Little Italy is making a visual claim for local hegemony. Today Chinese language characters, and the colors gold and red (good luck and prosperity) compete with Italian wrods, and the colors red, white, and green (Italian flag) for defining the ethnic identity of the street. The shop is located on a corner of 18th Avenue, which was renamed 'Cristoforo Colombo Boulevard' when the Italian American population was at its demographic and political apex. We might assume that, if demographic trends continue it might be renamed 'Confucius Way' in the future.

Figure 7.1 Wei's Gift Shop on Cristoforo Colombo Boulevard, Bensonhurst
Source: Author.

Other ways that one can see how Little Italies have changed is to look closely at events that are labeled as ethnically 'Italian' such as religious festivals. Ethnic change has come to the 'Italian' feast of Our Lady of Mount Carmel, which takes place every summer in what is left of New York's East Harlem Little Italy. Afro-Caribbean residents of New York City also venerate Our Lady of Mount Carmel and are now prominent participants in the annual event. We might consider whether the racial appearances of those who march in the parade challenge its meaning as an ethnic Italian event.

Figure 7.2 Flag bearers in Our Lady of Mount Carmel Parade, East Harlem, Manhattan

Source: Author.

There are also local businesses which to varying degrees have maintained a symbolic *Italianità* despite being located in the middle of neighborhoods dominated by other groups. For example, here is Claudio's Barber Shop in East Harlem, which at one time was Italian Harlem and is now Spanish Harlem. In fact there are today only one or two visibly Italian businesses on a street filled with hundreds of Latino (Dominican, Mexican, and Puerto Rican) shops. The Italian barber has been as ubiquitous a symbol of Italian neighborhoods, as have bakeries, delicatessens, and butchers selling Italian provisions. They are things we expect to see in Italian neighborhoods.

Figure 7.3 Claudio's Barber Shop on 116ᵗʰ Street, East Harlem, Manhattan
Source: Author.

In this photograph of the Marco Polo Restaurant in once Italian-dominated South Brooklyn we see a representation of a common genre of 'Italian-style' exterior commercial architecture in the form of Roman arches and the look of Roman ruins. Different sections of this neighborhood have experienced not only the influx of new ethnic groups such as Latinos and Middle Easterners but extensive gentrification and displacement of less affluent Italian-Americans as well. Now that the neighborhood is more upscale it is called 'Carroll Gardens'. These kinds of restaurants are making bold claims about their ethnic authenticity to mostly non-Italian patrons. In the old, perhaps even authentic, Italian American neighborhoods there were very few restaurants of this type as working-class families tended to eat at home.

Figure 7.4 The Marco Polo Restaurant, South Brooklyn (Carroll Gardens)
Source: Author.

Rome, Italy

It is beyond the scope of this paper to speculate as to the degree that the reality and or the image of Italy will change in response to immigration. Up to now and presently, the scale of immigration has been far less than an even a slow year for places like New York City. It does argue, however, that the ecological and semiotic processes of ethnic succession are quite similar. As might be expected there are also similarities between Italian and Italian American attitudes towards 'invaders'. As noted by Giuseppe Sciortino and Asher Colombo (2004) there is a pattern to the spatial distribution of immigrants to Italian regions which can be explained by work opportunities, geographical proximity, national and local policies and, not least, family and work networks. In Rome for example, the Chinese have established themselves in the restaurant business. I would argue that for all immigrant groups this same logic percolates downward to specific cities within regions, and then to specific areas in cities themselves.

Russell King and Jacqueline Andall's observations, as they were contemporaneous with my research in Rome, are also of value here. Commenting on increasing xenophobia towards, and political posturing about, non-EU foreigners they noted that:

> In very recent years the media frenzy has created powerful yet badly distorted images associating immigrants with widespread violence and crime. National stereotypes are repeated almost daily on television screens and in newspapers: crude associations between North Africans and drugs, Albanians and racketeering; black African women and prostitution. While some immigrants are undoubtedly engaged in criminal activities, the degree of association is vastly exaggerated, and much less prominence is given to Italians' engagement in crime, including that against immigrants. With barely 2.5 per cent of the population in Italy of immigrant origin, much less than in most other European countries, the 'crisis in immigration' is truly a crisis of (mis) representation. (1999, 155)

Rome had the third highest percentage of immigrants (5.5%), the largest absolute number (211, 200), and the greatest diversity of immigrant nationalities, of any province in Italy and might therefore be referred to 'as the capital of immigration'. They also noted changes in composition of immigrants from 1975 to 1997 and that the most rapid increases were in Asians and those from north and sub-Saharan African. North Africans increased from 1.9% to 17.7%, Asians from 3.8% to 15.7% and sub-Saharan Africans from 2.8% to 10.3%. For Romans, as for New Yorkers, immigration and changing neighborhoods are local as well as national political issues. Caritas reports on a survey of attitudes of Italians towards immigrants in 2002. In it they found that 72% of Italians expressed negative attitudes towards their new neighbors, and that there was a direct relationship level of education and hostility toward immigrants (Caritas 2003, 72).

My proposal in the early 1990s to come to Italy to lecture and research on how European urban landscapes might change in response to migration by using the American model of ethnic succession was met with amusement by my Italian social science colleagues. At that time the working assumption was that immigrant populations in Italy were temporary migrants not permanent residents. This attitude changed quickly because of regional and world events, which were in turn further accelerated by European Union expansion. As noted most recently by Natalia Magnani, in the theorizing by Italian researchers the idea of immigrants maintaining a separate ethnic identity upon which social divisions and social organization would develop in Italy was discounted (2005). It is therefore not unexpected that 'American' models of ethnic enclaves would also not be seen as useful.

Now we shall turn to the contemporary Italian urban scene where there is a related problem of visual transformation of the vernacular landscape. Here our focus will be on people as well as buildings. An important aspect of the city scene is the people in the picture. People become part of the space by simply being in it. Tourism is a major international industry and the sales image of Italy is derived in large part from foreigners' mental images of the public realms, spaces accessible to all (Lofland 1998), of Italians cities and towns. These spaces contain both monumental and vernacular landscapes. We might say that, for tourists at least, Italy itself is one huge multifaceted ethnic theme park. Millions of visitors flock to places like Rome every year with expectations about what the 'real' Italy and 'real' Italians look like. They come expecting to view an Italy that conforms to their stereotypical expectations.

Luckily for those who market the traditional images of Rome, few visitors travel outside the more ancient and historical center. Perhaps they pass through the central station and a few may occasionally ride on public transportation. During their sojourn they will see ethnically diverse crowds of tourists, but not much of the local population. While eating out they seldom will look beyond the dining room into restaurant kitchens. While making purchases at local stores they will not peek into the rear of shops to see the workers toiling there. In short they see only a small proportion of the public realm and the people who live in the city of Rome.

In 1991 the population of Rome was 2,775,250 and the percentage of foreigners with permission was 3.9%. By 1998 the population grew to 2,812,473 and registered foreigners were 4.8% of the population. Multiethnic Rome has residents from 167 different nations. Caritas estimated that in 1998 legal and illegal, temporary and permanent immigrants together were 6.2% of the Roman population. There were 134,578 foreign residents in Rome and an estimated 40,000 more who were unregistered (Caritas, 1998). In contrast, since 1900 New York City has averaged a foreign-born population of at least 30%. Further information provided by Caritas Roma on school children indicated that the immigrant populations were not randomly dispersed. As one might also anticipate this concentration mirrors the census data, which finds the highest concentration of immigrants in the center. Immigrants seem to be connected by major public transportation routes out from center to the northeast, north, northwest, and west.

Those who study immigration in Italy well understand that the published estimates of resident foreigners, as well as information about their origins, are not very reliable. The biggest problem is underestimation of the size of the population because of growing numbers of undocumented aliens (*clandestini*). This is further complicated in places like Rome by the large number of tourists and other foreign visitors. This makes visual sociological research of even greater value for the understanding of multiethnic Italian spaces where foreign populations are more visibly evident on the streets than would be anticipated by official statistics.

I quickly discovered that visual indications of immigrant concentration were not merely residential but in particular kinds of urban territory. After identifying those areas in which I expected to find immigrants I traveled to them by foot, bus, and subway. This is important to note because most immigrants, when not walking, regularly use public transportation. My first findings were made in transit. Immigrants make up a larger than expected proportion of those using public transportation, especially on certain routes. Their over-representation is enhanced by the fact that Italians carry on their romance with their cars and scooters by driving to work. Once I arrived at a designated 'immigrant' zone I spent hours walking the streets, some of which I revisited some several times.

Of all the districts which I observed and photographed the most 'visibly ethnic' was near the central station especially the western side and then southward. There, residence, work, shopping, and public transportation are concentrated. It is interesting to note that in general the center of the city with its pedestrian shopping areas and thousands of tourists is multi-ethnic, but not necessarily residentially mixed. Also, in the residences near the station there was a significant undercount of immigrants (many possibly *clandestini*), who share apartments with registered aliens and who may be sleeping in the same buildings in which they work. My street-level observations, as well as looking into private spaces behind normally closed doors, reveal a much larger immigrant world. Another problem for ethnographic researchers is that Italian residential spaces are difficult to access because they are usually set off from public spaces. Looking for indications of new immigrants around the central station in 1998 I observed a Little Africa, a growing Chinatown, and a flourishing Bengali jewelry trade. Both Chinatown and the jewelry markets seemed to also be light production centers; which would be consistent with undocumented alien workers in sweatshops. Local stores also displayed and sold ethnic foods, as well as other culturally appropriate services, provisions, and clothing. On my return in 2003 there seemed to be fewer Chinese but signs of the south Asian (Indian and Pakistani) population had significantly increased and a Moslem Middle Eastern (for example, Palestinian), presence was also more in evidence. There were contradictory signs of upscale gentrification as well as struggling immigrant populations. Ethnic changes, such as *halal* meat were evidenced in the local indoor public food market but the outdoor food market had disappeared. Clearly the Esquilino is part of Rome's zone of transition.

In previous papers (2003a and 2003b) I have identified the following situations, places, and activities in which ethnic differences were most visibly notable during my 1998 research in Rome: public transportation centers, major urban automobile routes, and centers of telecommunication such as public telephone banks or long distance telephone service outlets. In 2003 this remained the case. At that time, as well as in 2003, other than the Asian and African section (Esquilino) near the central station few areas in the city were widely recognized, or publicized, as having a distinctly ethnic identity in the sense that Americans speak of ethnic neighborhoods.

Just as the visual presence of different groups and uses of local spaces in Italian-American neighborhoods change their meanings a similar process is taking place in Italian cities. One ought to think of this set of photographs as another text about the contested meanings of Italianness. Perhaps the most iconic, or perhaps iconoclastic, image I have taken in my visits to L'Esquilino is one of the 'Little India Restaurant'. It shows a way of thinking about spaces in Italy that directly challenges the ownership of territory. One can also glimpse the linguistic as well as aesthetic challenge to the sacred 'Italian' city of Rome.

Figure 7.5 Little India Restaurant, L'Esquilino, Rome
Source: Author.

A common sight in America's ethnically defined neighborhoods are local businesses that provide ethnically appropriate provisions for local residents such as Italian or Spanish groceries. These businesses, which obviously cater to a distinct ethnic clientele, and perhaps even dissuade outsiders from entering, make a striking visible claim for local hegemony. The appearance therefore of an Indian grocery store in Rome says a great deal about local workers and inhabitants who would feel welcome and most comfortable there.

Figure 7.6 Indian grocery, L'Esquilino, Rome
Source: Author.

Another way of changing the ethnic sense of an area is by the language of signage. The L'Esquilino area is obviously defined by local businesses such as Chinese clothing stores and Bangladeshi jewelers. Not only are the aesthetics of the displays at great variance from the ways that one expects for Italian businesses to present themselves but they also frequently lack signage in Italian, which has a major impact on the ethnic 'feel' of the locale. It is in this way that locations like L'Esquilino become 'ethnic districts' and not merely Roman clothing or jewelry districts.

Figure 7.7 Bangladeshi jewelry store, L'Esquilino, Rome
Source: Author.

Figure 7.8 Chinese clothing store, L'Esquilino, Rome
Source: Author.

Summary

It can be said with confidence that immigrants (first and second generations) have been symbolically transforming the public spaces of Rome. As had their Italian immigrant counterparts to cities in the United States, immigrants to Rome have been gradually changing the vernacular landscapes by their own, merely physical, appearances as well as their activities in the spaces they use. Their presence and their 'difference' also change the value of the space. As have nonwhite migrants to American city neighborhoods, in some cases they have also stigmatized places by their presence (Krase 1977). It is interesting to note in this regard that some better-off Romans are beginning to flee the least desirable of the central zones citing classic urban dissatisfactions with changing inner city neighborhoods such as 'noise', 'dirt', and 'crime'. In contrast, at the same time that some residents move out, in other central Roman areas property values are soaring and what American urbanists would regard as 'gentrification' is taking place. This urban development paradox is not inconsistent with observations of David Harvey on 'circuits of capital' (1989).

In my first reports on my research in Rome I had asked the rhetorical question of when will the contribution of immigrants to the city's vernacular landscape be represented in tourist books and city guides. I have yet to see directions to Chinatown in Rome or bilingual Italian-Chinese street signs similar to those found in more established Chinatowns found in London, Paris, and New York. There are however other indications of the change such as in the following New York Times travel section article which for the first time incorporates the ethnic changes in Rome as part of the scene and scenery. The author, Michael Mewshaw, **comments on** many of the same spaces that I have observed on my many visits and photographic researches:

> But even in this quintessential Italian setting, I couldn't help noticing the presence of extracomunitari, as the immigrants are called. Every Sunday evening, Chiesa della Natività di Gesù throbs with the chants and clapping of Congolese Catholics. Two blocks away at Chiesa di San Tommaso Apostolo, Coptic Christians from Ethiopia and Eritrea fill the Via di Parione, with women in flowing robes and the sounds of drums and reed pipes, all of which provokes bafflement in early morning drinkers at the nearby Abbey Theater Pub. (2004, 12)

> As I emerged from San Silvestro, it occurred to me that a trek through Roman churches these days constitutes more than a promenade across the grand breadth and glorious length of city. It has become a microcosmic pilgrimage around the globe. Adding the Jewish Tempio Maggiore, the Islamic Moschea di Roma and the Rome Buddhist Vihara to the mix, anyone with energy and curiosity can now touch base with many of the world's major religions and races in a long day's walk. (13)

Another source of new multicultural meanings of stereotypically Italian tourist areas in Rome can be found here in a description of the Esquilino at an internet home exchange service (Homexchange.com) for the month of July, 2004:

The house is located in the lively, multiethnic, and safe neighbourhood of Esquilino. The Coliseum, S. Giovanni, S. Maria Maggiore are all within easy walking distance (15 minutes or less) , and metro, bus and tram stops are all within 100ft of the front door. 10 minutes' walk or two metro stops will take you to the central railway station.

The modern neighbourhood of Esquilino was built in the 1800s to accommodate the new administration officials for the Italian government after the military defeat of the Pope. It has now become the center of multiethnic Rome, with shops, restaurants, and services geared to serve a mixed clientele. As immigration to Italy is a fairly recent phenomenon, all foreign cultures retain the authenticity of their origins. (Rome, Italy Home ID# 35807)

Slowly but surely, the meanings of Rome's spaces are changing because of the transformation in the appearance of its vernacular landscapes. We have already rhetorically asked when will 'Chinatown', 'Little India', or 'Little Africa' become part of the tourist landscape, but even more critical is when will the meaning of 'Italian' include, to Italians as well as non-Italians, the racial and national diversity which is growing before their eyes? Such questions require much further discussion and certainly greater research efforts but they can be speculated upon here. What is clear is that these visual urban aesthetic encounters set in motion ecological and semiotic processes which lead to the social construction of real and imagined ethnic spaces and places.

Acknowledgement is made here to Rector's Committee for Scientific Research, and the Department of Sociology, University of Rome, La Sapienza for support of my photographic research on the 'New Immigrants to Rome', in 1998 and The Center for Italian Studies at State University of New York at Stony Brook for follow up study in 2003.

References

Alba, R.D., Crowder, K., and Logan, J.R. (1997), 'White Ethnic Neighborhoods and Assimilation: The Greater New York Region 1980–1990', *Social Forces* 75:3, 883–909.
Barthes, R. (1985), 'Day by Day with Roland Barthes', in Blonsky, M. (ed.).
Blonsky, M. (ed.) (1985), *On Signs* (Baltimore: Johns Hopkins Press).
Cannistraro, P.V. (ed.) (1999), *The Italians of New York: Five Centuries of Struggle and Achievement* (New York: New York Historical Society).
Caritas (1998), *Gli Studenti Stranieri nell'Area Romana, Forum per l'intercultura Promosso dalla Caritas Diocesana di Roma, Centro Studi & Documentazione* (April).
Caritas (2003), *Dossier Statistico Immigrazione 2002* (Roma: Nuova Anterem).
Castells, M. (1989), *The Informational City* (Oxford: Blackwell).
Davis, M. (2001), *Magical Urbanism: Latinos Reinvent the U.S. City* (London: Verso).
Gardaphe, F.L. (1996), *Italian Signs, American Streets: The Evolution of Italian*

American Narrative (Durham: Duke University Press).

Gottdiener, M. (1994), *The Social Production of Urban Space*, 2nd ed. (Austin: University of Texas Press).

Grady, J. (1996), 'The Scope of Visual Sociology', *Visual Sociology*. 11:2, 10–24.

Gutiérrez, D.G. (1999), 'Migration, Emergent Ethnicity, and the 'Third Space': The Shifting Politics of Nationalism in Greater Mexico', *Journal of American History* 86:2, 481–517.

Harvey, D. (1989), *The Urban Experience* (Baltimore: Johns Hopkins University Press).

Hayden, D. (1991) 'The Potential of Ethnic Places for Urban Landscapes', *Places* 7:1, 11–17.

Jackson, J.B. (1984), *Discovering the Vernacular Landscape* (New Haven: Yale University Press).

King, R. and Andall, J. (1999), 'The Geography and Economic Sociology of Recent Immigration to Italy', *Modern Italy* 4:2, 135–58.

Krase, J. (1977), 'Reactions to the Stigmata of Inner City Living', *Journal of Sociology and Social Welfare* 4:7, 997–1011.

Krase, J. (1993), 'Traces of Home', *Places: A Quarterly Journal of Environmental Design* 8:4, 46–55.

Krase, J. (1997), 'The Spatial Semeiotics of Little Italies and Italian Americans' in Toscano A.M. (ed.).

Krase, J. (1999) 'New York City's Little Italies: Yesterday, Today – and Tomorrow?' in Cannistraro, P.V. (cd.).

Krase, J. (2002), 'Navigating Ethnic Vernacular Landscapes Then and Now', *Journal of Architecture and Planning Research* 19:4, 274–281.

Krase, J. (2003a), 'Imagining Italians and Others: Sharing Public Space', paper presented at Italians Diasporas Share the Neighbourhood. The Europeans Program. Perth. The University of Western Australia.

Krase, J. (2003b), 'Italian and Italian American Identity', illustrated paper presented at the Merica: convegno sulla cultura e letteratura degli italiani del nordamerica. Rome.

Krase, J. (2004), 'Italian American Urban Landscapes: Images of Social and Cultural Capital', *Italian Americana* 22:1, 17–44.

Lefebvre, H. (1991), *The Production of Space* (Oxford: Blackwell).

Lofland, L. (1998), *The Public Realm: Exploring the City's Quintessential Social Territory* (New York: Aldine de Gruyter).

Magnani, N. (2005), 'Migration, New Urban Ethnic Minorities and the Race/ Ethnic Relations Approach in a Recent Immigration Country: The Case of Italy', unpublished paper.

Mewshaw, M. (2004), 'In Churches, A Mosaic of Cultures', The New York Times, travel section, 27 June, 12–13.

Park, R.E., Burgess, E.W., and McKensie, R.D. (1925), *The City* (Chicago: University of Chicago Press).

Sciortino, G. and Colombo, A. (2004), 'Italian Immigration: The Origins, Nature

and Evolution of Italy's Migratory Systems', *Journal of Modern Italian Studies*
    9:1, 49–70.
Toscano, M.A. (ed.) (1997), *Dialettica Locale-Globale* (Napoli: Impermedium).

Internet-based references

'Rome, Italy Home ID#35807', (published online 2003) <http://www.Homeexchange.
    com>.

Chapter 8

Working in the Skyline – Images and Everyday Action

Lars Meier

Seeing and acting in the skyline – introduction

The everyday encounters of German bankers with different places in London are explored in this chapter. In their encounters with the City of London and with Brixton, the seemingly 'placeless global elite' (see Castells 1996; Sklair 2001; Bauman 2000) feels the power of place in their everyday life in London.

Places are entangled with different meanings and images. In their everyday life the mobile bankers must interact not only with concrete material in the form of particular architecture, but also with their specific, preconceptualized images of the scene. With the title 'Working in the skyline' I am referring to the interactions between everyday practices and specific meanings which are ascribed to unique places; places in which the practices are in turn grounded. Images of places are entangled with everyday activity, too. They influence concrete encounters with the materiality of the place, with its rhythm, and with other people acting there. The bankers are not only viewing the skyline, they are also acting *in* the skyline (e.g. working, walking, talking) in the concrete place.

A short discussion of the concepts of place and landscape will illuminate the ways in which the interconnections between images, everyday acts, and structure are laid out in this chapter. My preference in using the notion of place instead of landscape is based on some reservations, or, in my opinion, limits to the use of the concept of landscape (see also Cresswell 2003). Landscape indicates a distant view from above and a more solid and unchangeable scene; it suggests an already painted image. Place is a concept which is more grounded and open to concrete action. It is tangible, furnished with materiality and with people; it is where encounters happen. Despite these limits however, analyses of landscapes are providing convincing insights into the character of images that are used in this chapter to explore the concrete encounters in the place.

Landscapes are by no means only natural or physical entities – they are complex sites of socially constructed meanings (see for example Duncan and Ley 1993;

Barnes and Duncan 1992). Edward Said (1978) shows this with the Orient. He points out that the 'Orient' is a product of the European imagination. This means that it is read from a specific perspective (in the case of the Orient, from a western imperialistic perspective). This specific reading (its imagination) of the Middle East as being exotic and mystical is a powerful product of western domination.

> Just as none of us is outside or beyond geography, none of us is completely free from the struggle over geography. That struggle is complex and interesting because it is not only about soldiers and cannons but also about ideas, about forms, about images and imaginings. (Said 1994, 6)

The image of a landscape is the result of a social contest about meanings. But it not only reflects the dominant position of power: in their unquestioned (seemingly natural) role, landscapes also naturalize ideologies (Duncan and Duncan 1988) and legitimize the powerful. Continuous contestation makes the image unstable. Therefore the image of a landscape can change from time to time. For example the way the bohemian image of the Docklands in East London changed, together with the transformation of the Docks, from 'a symbol of the nation's dark side' (Eade 2000, 124), an exotic other which was characterized by Jack the Ripper, danger and filth, to a clean and developed 'state of the art financial and commercial center' (Eade 1997, 132) after the 1980s.

The perception of a landscape, the inscribed image, is not entirely monolithic. It also depends on the social identity of the one who perceives the landscape. The 'Orient' is viewed from a western perspective, the filthy and dangerous Docks from a bohemian perspective, and women's fear of specific urban spaces and their image of these places as dangerous is also not necessarily reflected in men's fear of the same place (see Smith 1989; Pain 1997). Landscapes can be viewed and imaged in different ways. But overall the image of the landscape is not only a type of reading experience; it is also a consequence of the process of writing (e.g. building). In this process, by structuring the landscape (e.g. arranging a specific architecture) the powerful suggest a specific reading: the dominant ideology is inscribed. Members of the dominant groups, such as the German bankers as members of the so called 'transnational capitalist class', can be seen as inscribing the dominant ideology and defining the normal (Jackson and Penrose 1993). The view of the German bankers who are working in the City of London is not global or universal, it is recognized as a specific view. It is taken from a particular perspective of a member of a specific social milieu of a specific national and ethnic identity (predominantly male) – it is taken from the perspective of white German bankers.

This chapter is concerned with unfolding the way in which German bankers are imaging the landscapes of the City and Brixton, and illuminating the intertwinedness of these images with their everyday activity, which is grounded there. In using the notion of place, I am pointing out that their everyday practices and encounters cannot be reduced to the processes of their reading and writing of the landscape. The images are analyzed as being part of the concrete encounters with the place, its specific structure, e.g. its materiality and atmosphere, which are consequences of a specific history and of its social, economic and political structures. Or, as Henri Lefebvre points out, places are 'characterized by a spatiality that is in fact irreducible to the mental realm' (Lefebvre 1991, 62).

By analyzing the interactions between their everyday activity and their ascription of meaning to two different places in London – in the City of London and in the south city quarter of Brixton – the significance of the local for everyday action of the so called 'global elite' is pointed out (see Meier 2006a; Meier 2006b). Grounding the activity of the high-flying global elite, or more precisely of the German bankers, their encounters with the real urban place are analyzed.

Researching place-based encounters of the global elite – method and data

Researching images, everyday actions, and encounters with urban places, this chapter is based on the findings of ethnographic research on German bank managers working and living in London. Besides conducting semi-structured interviews with nineteen bankers, their sense of place is analyzed using field-notes from participant observations in the City and in Brixton, places which have a specific significance in the everyday life of the bankers. By observing these places (their materiality, structure, and atmosphere) the particular banker's views of their everyday places (as determined by the interview sequences) are confronted and integrated with the researcher's view of these places. By taking photographs of the places and recording the interactions in these places, the view of the researcher and his encounters with these places are being intertwined with an analysis of the banker's view of their encounters with these places. The photographs are illustrations of the text: of the interview sequences and of my analysis. They add to the text and support the reader with an expanded impression of the places and encounters. In combination with the text, they can direct the reader's view to the specific encounters of the German bankers with the City and with Brixton.

Working in the City of London

On each daily arrival in the City of London (the City), the German financial managers view the skyline of the City. Specific images are impressed upon their vision, which they attribute to the City. The following interview sequence, describing a banker's daily arrival in the City, gives an impression of this image:

> If you go over the London Bridge to the City, looking right one sees the Tower Bridge, looking forward you see the City built in front of you and then you walk into it. For me that is quite impressive, the compact City, the square mile you see directly compact in front of you ... and you also see such a historical building like the Tower Bridge on the one side and St. Paul's to the left and then you go into the center of the economy. (L18, 383–91)[1]

---

1   The interview sequences are marked by assigned codes for different interviewees (e.g. S5).

Figure 8.1 Skyline of the City
Source: Author.

The City appears as 'the center of the economy' (L18), a center whose importance seems heightened in the view of the bankers by their perception of special buildings which are signs for a historically based importance of the City. 'Tower Bridge and the Tower, these are quite impressive buildings. It's not that I go there gladly, but if you are there then it is impressive' (L18, 649).

The City could not be seen by the bank managers without their view being 'impressed' upon by historical buildings. These buildings are not only credentials of the current centrality of the City 'as the center of the economy' (L18) for the German bankers. If this were the case then the City could be perceived by a view of the few skyscrapers in London, of the futuristic glass Swiss Re building designed by Renzo Piano, of the colorfully illuminated Lloyds of London at night, of Tower 42 or of the NatWest tower, buildings that are not mentioned in the bankers' statements. Their perceptions of the skyline, the view of St. Paul's Cathedral but not of the Swiss Re building, indicate that the bankers are imaging the City, 'the center of the economy' (L18), in its tradition as a center of the British Empire. Their view is concentrated on buildings that could be seen as materialized evidence of the historically grounded importance of the City of London as the former center of the British Empire. Looking at St. Paul's, the bankers are looking at a building that was able to resist the German bombing in World War II and that became a symbol of British survival, of the persistent strength and indestructible durability of the City (Daniels 1993). The cathedral of St. Paul's refers also, like Tower Bridge, to the British Empire: here is the tomb of Lord Nelson and the wedding place of Prince Charles and Lady Di. St. Paul's is regarded in Britain as the 'Heart of the Empire' (Daniels 1993, 15).

This view of the German bankers is guided by the skyline planning efforts of the Corporation of London. Their aim was to preserve and enhance a specific skyline of the City. By decree, regulations regarding the height of new buildings ensured that the view of St. Paul's from different points around the city would be preserved (see Jacobs 1996, 47–50).

The German bankers specifically perceive buildings that reflect the history of the City and stand for its tradition as the colonial center (Tower Bridge) and for its everlasting strength (St. Paul's). The City in this view seems to be historically grounded and affirmed as 'the center of the economy' (L18) as *the* center, marked by its traditional centrality and its high international importance, which the German bankers emphasize with by a comparison with other financial centers. Thus an interviewee says: 'Frankfurt is not the navel of the world, that is rather London.' (L8, 30)

The experience of arriving in the City and beginning to work is equivalent to personally profiting from the image of the City as 'the navel of the world' (L8). Being successful enough to work in the hub of the world is seen as a personal achievement and advancement. The image of the globally important and successful center of control, the City, is transferred to the own self. After leaving the City, it is manifested in the curriculum vitae as a competitive advantage.

> Clearly I wanted to do something for my CV. Because as a rule one leaves for 2 years and after returning one automatically enters a higher position. That is completely clear. Thus for the CV this is very important, that will be admitted by everyone. See, I stand by it. (L6, 119)

For the German financial manager, arriving in the City becomes an experience of personal success, a rite of initiation through which one becomes a part of *the* center. With the entrance into the city the image of international importance and centrality, which the managers ascribe to the skyline of the City, is reflected back on the self:

> Then I drove from the south to the north over Waterloo Bridge. On the right side you see the city of London, on the left side you see Big Ben and the Houses of Parliament. That is a moment where I thought: It is so great to work in the City. It is so impressive that I made it, that I can work in the City. ... That was the key experience for me and then I said to myself, I fit exactly into this city. (L14, 72–76)

Because the City is being imagined by the financial manager as important, as the center, the self is aligned with the image of City, with its characteristics – one 'fit[s] exactly into this city' (L14). Personal characteristics such as courage, determination, readiness to perform, and adaptability are attributes that the financial managers ascribe to themselves. Having these attributes is the financial employee's explanation for winning the competition for a job in the city. One interviewee said: 'Everybody wants to go to London. This is selected in advance, one fits the profile, fits the request.' (L10, 50–54)

Working in the City, moving through its skyline, is aligned with success and the promise of gain for the future career, which is the reason for subordinating previous plans. An interviewee told me:

> I expected to go to Frankfurt or to Munich, this was my expectation. I didn't intend to go to London. But as I said, the phone call was a nice surprise. Then it needed a little

conviction and is difficult to say … Okay actually we wanted to move in together, one apartment my fiancée and I, instead it goes apart into different directions. (L1, 109–12)

The capability for adaptation appears in the narrations of the German financial managers as a main characteristic with which one must comply to be part of the City. They describe their everyday life in the City as comprehensive adaptation to the specific daily rhythm of the city.

During the week, in the morning from 7 o'clock, men in dark suits and women in dark costumes walk with a fast and very purposeful stride from the Tube and railway stations into the City, avoiding eye contact on the way. At this time, the city quarter seems to be dominated by finance employees, who want to reach their offices as quickly as possible without being disturbed by their surroundings. An interviewee said: 'Try to smile at someone, you will get rarely a smile back.' (L1, 375)

That 321,000 individuals (International Financial Services 2005) are working here in a tight area, where only 7,000 live, is tangible for the German bankers every morning and evening. One interviewee says:

I arrive with very very many people, if I am coming in to the City. There are *streams of humans* coming to the city, because the people are coming from far outside. London is a metropolis, that means all the people are streaming through the city, in the morning into it and in the evening out. (L4, 339–41)

Figure 8.2 Streams of humans, bankers on their way to work in the morning near Bank

Source: Author.

The German bankers feel themselves as part of the streams into the City. They are carried away by the streams, their own movements adapting to the movement in the City. With thousands of others, they are walking quite purposefully and quickly along the pavement. To hesitate or to pause seems to be inappropriate, the narrowness of the pavements and the absence of resting places (such as parks or benches) make the one that hesitates an obstacle to the 'streams of humans' (L4).

The largest part of their working day is described by the financial managers as being a continuous process of communication: with the headquarters in Germany, with customers worldwide, or especially in face to face contact in the City, which explains the steady movements on the streets.

Figure 8.3 Bankers in motion
Source: Author.

These localized face to face contacts are suggested by the specific structure of the City: its high density, the specialized infrastructure like the omnipresent cafes, restaurants, sandwich bars, pubs and business clubs. One interviewee describes this in his own words:

> The contact between the banks here in London is very intensive and of course you often see the others and meet them, it is not a journey. You know that here in the City everything is normally reachable by foot, and therefore you are often on your way by foot. (L19, 72)

Regarding the lunch break, the German financial managers often miss the German canteen. In the City it is replaced by a more hectic midday food supply, and the Germans are adapting their usual eating behaviors:

> You have hundreds of thousands of sandwich bars here in the City, where you quickly guzzle something down. Alone or quickly with a colleague who has time, who says come with me, I am on my way to get a sandwich. In the summer, you can sit outside at a green corner, if you can find it or you are going into the office and are eating at your workplace. Unfortunately, this is the culture here. And if it goes wrong you are writing your emails while you are eating your sandwich. (L11, 140–48)

The German financial managers are not only adjusting themselves to the unfamiliar culture of eating in the City, expressed by their reliance on the countless sandwich shops. They are also changing their style of clothing compared to Germany. The male finance employees adapt themselves to the clothing style in the City: they do not wear light colored suits like they did in Germany; in the City the dark suit is the norm. If they do not already own dark suits they buy them for their stay in the City. Variations in clothes are limited only to the color of the shirts, to the often multicolored ties and to the choice of cuff-links. All wear their hair cut short and most have trained bodies, which they form in the gyms of the City.

In their clothes, but also in their brisk and purposeful motion through the City, they differentiate themselves from other people who also working in the same space: from the blue dressed men who are emptying the trash can, from the people employed in the Starbucks branches dressed in green smocks and standing behind the bar, from the road cleaning forces, the taxi and delivery drivers, bicycle couriers, construction workers, security firm employees, and the employees of the bars and restaurants – all of these other working groups are invisible to the extent that they do not play a role in the everyday narrations of the German bank employees.

The City imparts the impression that everything is aligned to keep the financial services running smoothly. An interviewee said to me: 'Everything lives according to the banks and the people who are working here, it is really only geared to serve that; during the day and perhaps for a few drinks in the evening.' (L15, 298)

Irritations to everyday business by the visibility of socially disadvantaged groups do not occur for the finance employees. The sidewalks in the City are partly private property of the office building owners – loiterers are easily driven out by the private security guards. In addition, there are only very limited public seats, which would invite people to stay for a while. Through this specific configuration, the City ensures that the finance employees are not disturbed in their fast routes through the City. Their perceptions of people not working in the financial sector are for these reasons very limited.

On the streets of the City and in the abandoned offices, the cleaners in their green uniforms are present after 8 pm. Only a few people in business suits or costumes are walking through the streets. A bank manager said:

It is like it is deserted in the evening and during the weekend too. That is a little bit weird, a little bit strange, because one knows about other big cities where there is more action in the evening, but when people go home after work it is a deserted city. (L4: 427)

On Saturday and on Sunday the City is almost completely deserted. Besides some tourists there are only a few construction and relocation workers.

Figure 8.4 Relocation helpers on Saturday in the City
Source: Author.

Figure 8.5 Street in the City on Saturday
Source: Author.

All bars, restaurants, and office buildings are closed. One interviewee said:

> During the week, the finance sector is crowded and during the weekend completely
> abandoned, therefore you don't see a human being on the street, everything is closed, no
> supermarket and no sandwich shop is open. It is really dead here. (L12, 268–70)

The financial managers coming from Germany to the City of London are adapting
themselves not only in their clothes and their daily routine to the everyday rhythms
and their images of the City of London as *the* center; they are also feeling the hectic
atmosphere of the place, the fast-paced movements on the street and in the trading
rooms. This specific kind of movement in the City affects the self of the German
financial managers. As I have demonstrated, they describe themselves as part of the
currents of humans which are streaming into the city: as part of the stream they adapt
to the rapid movements, they adapt themselves by not accepting a calm lunch; they
advise jaywalking, crossing red lights, and maintaining a gaze which does not cross
the gaze of others.

They also lose sight of other social groups in the City. Although these are
necessary for the functioning of the City, their relevance is not displayed in the
everyday references of the German financial managers. In the City, one sees oneself
as part of the group of successful financial managers: if these leave the City in the
evening, then the city, although there are blue collar workers, is seen as being dead.

Accordingly, the financial managers take note of the City predominantly as a functional place for the finance business, as a functional place of global centrality.

Passing through Brixton

In driving through the city, often on the way from the southwest borough of Richmond,[2] the German bankers pass through Brixton. Normally this city quarter has no relevance in the concrete everyday life of the bankers; for them it is not a popular place.

The German finance managers encounter the southern London city quarter of Brixton, which is part of the Borough of Lambeth, with completely different conceptions from their conceptions of the City. Their narrations and their behavior differ substantially from that in the City. One interviewee said:

> L11: There are really areas, where one said in former times, the daggers are flying low. Nowadays I only drive through with locked doors. Especially when you pass by at night or in the evening: that's Brixton, that's East London, that's not nice and that's not safe.

> I: Did you have some experiences there?

> L11: I, no ... Well that some dubious figures knocked on the car-window, but then you hit the throttle and you pass on through. Still, nothing happened to me, but if one hears about things happening, it is predominantly in these areas. (L11, 261–64)

Without having been in Brixton in a worrying situation, often even without ever having been in Brixton, the banker is ascribing danger to the place. This is of particular importance for the behavior of the financial managers in Brixton. The finance employees try to evade the ascribed threat by avoiding close contact with the inhabitants. They not only avoid walking on the street and coming into contact with residents, but also even passing through and getting within sight of the ascribed threat. An interviewee told me:

> In Brixton I drive through reluctantly in the evening, with the motorbike I don't mind, cause you are relatively flexible, but with the car. Because I am a car freak and having a car which doesn't look bad. Then they scratch along the car and wait for you leaving the car. The automatic reaction is 'Mein heiliges Blechle' [a German impression of anger or shock] and than he leaves the car and while he leaves someone else gets in the car and drives away. Then you can go home by foot. And for them this is just an object of utility, which they throw away somewhere. (L13, 492–98)

Another financial manager said:

---

2   Richmond is a preferred residential area for the German bankers. It is a green, upmarket residential area near the Thames and near the German School (Meier 2006a).

> Where I rarely go is Brixton in South London. There are I believe 70 to 80 per cent blacks, there I feel in a minority. That does not mean that I am basically afraid there, but because of these clearly superior numbers I feel uncomfortable. (L14, 536)

Although 64% of Brixton's population are white and only 26% are black (National Statistics Census 2001), the financial managers consider this residential area as being a neighborhood dominated by blacks. Parallel to this, the ascription of blackness is linked with an ascription of danger, which is then transferred to the city quarter: for the German bank managers Brixton is a black city quarter and therefore it is imagined as dangerous. This interrelation between blackness and threat shows in the following interview excerpt where one interviewee differentiates Indians from blacks: 'There are frictions in specific areas, where there is a higher fraction of foreigners. Blacks, Indians not as much, but Blacks yes, if you go for example to Brixton.' (L11, 184)

The image of threat bound to Brixton connects the finance manager directly with their ascription of blackness as being one with danger and disrespect. Accordingly, they are afraid of getting into danger in Brixton; the idea of staying there is associated with a feeling of unease. 'If you look at someone in the wrong way there, then you have to worry that people consciously walk around the area looking for someone strange, just to stir up trouble.' (L1: 439)

The managers also fear that the blacks, imaged as being disrespectful and naive, are not competent in dealing with the cultural goods of the whites and that they treat a valuable car as a disposable object:

> Earlier when I lived in the South East, there where some roads where I said on the way: Here you don't want to break down. That is for example Brixton, an area where many Caribbean people live. There the police found my pinched car. The thief had pinched it just because he wanted to transport a fridge, so the police said. (L13, 484)

Some of the German financial managers are going to Brixton in spite of the ascribed danger. For them this is an exotic adventure: discovering the foreign.

> I don't avoid going out to Brixton or into areas which are not so amazing. Recently, I went to the market in Brixton. Just to look at it (L4, 685–87).

Figure 8.6 Road scene at the Brixton Market
Source: Author.

By accepting and confirming this adventure, attributes are reproduced which are – from the perspective of the banker – attributes that are also required for being successful in the City: they must be bold, without fear, curious, and adaptable. This adaptation takes a different form because different images are brought into the City and into Brixton.

From the perspective of the bank employees, going to Brixton is only possible if one has the skill of dealing in the right way with the danger inscribed here. Elija Anderson showed that the feeling of danger depends on how familiar one is with the neighborhood. The bankers who are entering Brixton are doing this only when they feel they have the ability to adapt to the correct behavior, or, in Anderson's terms, they are employing a 'street etiquette' (Elijah Anderson 1990), which is seen as a necessary protection against expected unpleasant encounters. 'I try to be as relaxed as possible, I go there to the cinema sometimes, but I try to avoid parking my car there. I don't know maybe not obviously spending money there. You are more careful there.' (L14, 534–36)

Another interviewee told me: 'If you give the impression of knowing the area, of knowing where you want to go. If you are searching for some place, then you are a potential victim. Hello here I am: the victim.' (L4, 699–701)

Street etiquette is a set of rules one formulates and applies in each situation. 'This requires only a generalized perception of the people one encounters, based on the most superficial characteristics.' (Anderson 1990, 210) Anderson distinguishes between street etiquette and the more sophisticated approach of 'street wisdom'. 'In achieving the wisdom that every public trial is unique, they become aware that individuals, not types, define special events.' (Anderson 1990, 230) Without having these insightful experiences of street wisdom, the German bankers are stuck in their generalizing images of Brixton. With a mix of ascriptions – dangerousness, being exotic, foreignness, and blackness – the German bank managers encounter Brixton. Their everyday behavior in the place, their feeling of discomfort, the quick passage through it, and the avoidance of contact, is caused to a large degree by these images. Experiences which do not fit these powerful images are not reported by them.

It is similar for the white, German, academic field researcher: the picture of the dense exotic market (Figure 8.6), which I shot and selected for this chapter is an expression of my specific view and of the images with which I encountered Brixton. These do not suggest a presentation of Brixton with a photo of the cinema Ritzy (at that time, I shot the photo not for research but because I liked the way the scenery looked, without thinking that I could use it for my work).

Figure 8.7 Ritzy
Source: Author.

My own feeling of being a foreigner in Brixton and my feeling of participating in a small adventure has an impact on my perspective and on my encounters with the specific place, as it has on the perspective of the German bankers.

Conclusion

In this chapter the intertwining of images of places and everyday action in these places has been analyzed. The everyday activity of German financial managers, their movements, clothes, and eating styles are in constant interaction with structures of places: with their architecture, infrastructure, daily rhythm, with 'others', and with the images that the financial managers are bringing to the place. By 'working in the skyline' the German bank managers are not only imaging the skyline based on images that they brought from elsewhere and then impressed into the skyline, they are also acting in the skyline, in the concrete place. It has been demonstrated that the specific images are translated into specific actions.

By encountering the City of London the bankers experience '*the* center of the economy' as demanding an adaptation of their selves to the place. Encountering the 'unsafe', 'exotic', 'black' Brixton also brings a feeling of necessary adaptation, although in a quite different way. In Brixton, the adaptation, getting the 'street etiquette', seems to be imperfect for the bankers. By being in Brixton they have to deal with their feelings of insecurity and anxiety. In the City they see themselves as perfectly fitting, as a part of the center.

References

Anderson, E. (1990), *Streetwise. Race, Class and Change in an Urban Community* (Chicago: University of Chicago Press).

Anderson, K. *et al.* (eds) (2003), *Handbook of Cultural Geography* (London: Sage).

Barnes, T. and Duncan, J. (eds) (1992), *Writing Worlds. Discourses, Text and Metaphor in the Representation of Landscape* (London: Routledge).

Bauman, Z. (2000), *Liquid Modernity* (Cambridge, UK: Polity Press).

Berking, H. *et al.* (eds) (2006), *Negotiating Urban Conflicts. Interaction, Space and Control* (Bielefeld: Transcript Verlag).

Castells, M. (1996), *The Rise of the Network Society* (Oxford: Blackwell Publishers).

Cresswell, T. (2003), 'Landscape and the Obliteration of Practice', in Anderson, K. *et al.* (eds).

Daniels, S. (1993), *Fields of Vision – Landscape Imagery and National Identity in England and the United States* (Cambridge, UK: Polity Press).

Duncan, J. and Duncan, N. (1988), '(Re)reading the Landscape' *Environment and Planning D. Society and Space* 6, 117–26.

Duncan, J. and Ley, D. (eds) (1993), *Place/Culture/Representation* (London: Routledge).

Eade, J. (1997), 'Reconstructing Places – Changing Images of Locality in Docklands and Spitalfields', in Eade, J. (ed.).

Eade, J. (ed.) (1997), *Living the Global City – Globalization as a Local Process*

(London: Routledge).

Eade, J. (2000), *Placing London – From Imperial Capital to Global City* (New York: Berghahn Books).

Evans, D.J. and Herbert, D.T. (eds) (1989), *The Geography of Crime* (London: Routledge).

Jacobs, J.M. (1996), *Edge of Empire – Postcolonialism and the City* (London: Routledge).

Jackson, P. and Penrose, J. (eds) (1993), *Constructions of Race, Place and Nation* (London: University College London Press).

Kreutzer, F. and Roth, S. (eds) (2006), *Transnationale Karrieren – Biographien, Lebensführung und Mobilität* (Wiesbaden: VS Verlag).

Lefebvre, H. (1991), *The Production of Space* (Oxford: Blackwell).

Meier, L. (2006a), 'Den Ort spüren, Distanz erfahren – Irritationen alltäglicher Handlungen deutscher Finanzbeschäftigter in London', in Kreutzer, F. and Roth, S. (eds).

Meier, L. (2006b), 'On the Road to Being White – The Construction of Whiteness in the Everyday Life of Expatriate German High Flyers in Singapore and London', in Berking, H. *et al.* (eds).

Pain, R.H. (1997), 'Social Geographies of Women's Fear of Crime', *Transactions of the Institute of British Geographers* 22, 231–44.

Said, E. (1978), *Orientalism. Western Conceptions of the Orient* (Harmondsworth: Penguin).

Said, E. (1994), *Culture and Imperialism* (London: Vintage).

Sklair, L. (2001), *The Transnational Capitalist Class* (Oxford: Blackwell Publishers).

Smith, S.J. (1989), 'The Fear of Crime in Britain', in Evans, D.J. and Herbert, D.T. (eds).

Internet-based references

'National Statistics Census 2001 - Brixton Hill Area Profil' (published online) <http: neighbourhood.statistics.gov.uk/dissemination/AreaProfile1.do?tab=2>, accessed 8 May 2006.

'International Financial Services - 2005 London - City Indicators Bulletin August 2005' (published online) <www.ifsl.org.uk>, accessed 8 May 2006.

Chapter 9

Simulation or Hospitality –
Beyond the Crisis of Representation in
Nowa Huta

Łukasz Stanek

Nowa Huta is a city founded in 1949 near Kraków, historically the Polish capital. The city was built as a prestige project of the new communist government to accommodate the workers of the simultaneously constructed steelworks, and since then the future of the city was tightly tied to that of the factory, which provided the inhabitants with work, social infrastructure, organized leisure, and a sense of identity and belonging. Since 1989 Nowa Huta has been transforming from a corporate city defined by production to a place shaped by other types of work and new forms of consumption.[1] The shrinking of the steelworks corresponds with the proliferation of malls and entertainment complexes which fill the empty spaces between Nowa Huta and Kraków, while the layoffs in the factory are paralleled by the growing importance of working places in non-productive sectors of the formal and informal economies.[2] Yet the production in Nowa Huta was not confined to the steelworks – the communist regime guaranteed a constant demand not only for steel, but also for the second product of Nowa Huta: the mass media representations of a happy, young, wealthy, modern 'socialist city'. Nowa Huta was founded by the communist regime as a projection of an idealized 'socialist city', and its literary, journalistic, photographic, and cinematic representations were disseminated throughout Poland. Even after Nowa Huta ceased to be an independent city (it was incorporated into Kraków in 1951, and in 1991 was divided into five districts) these representations kept influencing both the physical transformations of the district and its everyday use. After the political and economic changes of 1989, Nowa Huta has been transforming

---

1   For a critical discussion of the thesis of 'end of work' and the changed importance of work in shaping everyday life in Nowa Huta after 1989; see Stenning 2003; 2005a; 2005b; 2005c.

2   The second largest workplace in Nowa Huta is Tomex, a bazaar. Recent studies also show the importance of informal economies in the lives of the inhabitants; see Stenning 2005d.

from a place where representations are produced to one in which they are consumed, mobilized in the tourist and city-marketing campaigns. The aim of the paper is to describe some of the new tendencies in dealing with representations of Nowa Huta in the transitory period of the early twenty-first century.

The relationships between practices of representation of space and other practices of production of space – material, political, and quotidian – were studied by Henri Lefebvre, whose theory of the production of space is the theoretical framework for this paper. According to Lefebvre, space is a product of various practices that is being transformed in material ways, represented in various media and for various purposes, and appropriated in everyday life. The relationship between these three types of practice (the material, the representational, and the quotidian practices) and the three aspects of space they produce (the perceived, conceived, and lived space) is itself worked out in social practice. The theory of production of space allows conceiving representations of space as penetrating all three levels distinguished by Lefebvre: not only the private level of everyday life and the global level of the market, state and mass culture, but also the 'mixed, mediating, or intermediary level' (2003, 80), where the two others interfere.[3] In this paper, I would like to focus on the influence of the representations of space on the intermediate level, which, as stated by Lefebvre, 'is the specifically urban level' (2003, 80). This influence is particularly crucial in Nowa Huta, because what today are the five districts of Kraków referred to as 'Nowa Huta' are a series of competing representations strongly embedded in various social practices and experiences rather than administrative or spatial delineations. I would like to investigate the importance of representations of space in Nowa Huta by focusing on the ways these representations were mobilized in a series of cultural, commercial, and political events in the city in the last five years, and by analyzing the roles and conventions these mobilizations imposed on the participating inhabitants and visitors, shaping their self-perception in urban space and the ways it is used. Analyzing Nowa Huta, the paper aims at contributing to Lefebvre's project of investigating the functions of representations of space in social practices, paying special attention to the interdependences between representations of space and power relations. These interdependences in Nowa Huta underwent a massive change after the collapse of communism, when the duel between the regime, imposing a propagandistic image of Nowa Huta; and its opponents, who answered with the production of subversive stories, were replaced by multipolar tensions between the administrative, commercial, and cultural powers (which instrumentalize isolated representations of the city) and those groups of inhabitants who oppose such instrumentalization. This paper positions the practices of representing space in this changed field of forces.

---

3   For the discussion about the question of levels and scales in Lefebvre's theory, compare Brenner 2000.

The crisis of representation of Nowa Huta after 1989

The clashes between the official propagandistic discourse and the subversive story-telling practices, which took place under communism, left Nowa Huta with a set of contradictory representations that were decisive for the discussion on the city after the political change and the abolition of censorship. Investigation into the representations of Nowa Huta in local newspapers and magazines between 1989 and 2002 reveals that all the representations were inherited from the communist period. Most importantly, the image of the 'first socialist city in Poland' and the city of decreed atheism was contrasted with the representation of Nowa Huta as the center of political opposition and impulsive Catholicism. Other influential representations, originally endowed with asynchronous temporalities and divergent rhythms, collapsed in the local mass media after 1989 into clear-cut oppositions. The representation of Nowa Huta as an integral part of Kraków was opposed by the accusation that the 'proletarian city' was located as hostile to the 'bourgeois Kraków'. Since the majority of the inhabitants were of rural origin, the city's industrial character was contrasted with its social structure, summarized as a 'big village'. The ecological catastrophe caused by the steelworks was juxtaposed with the reputation of Nowa Huta as the 'greenest district of Kraków'. Since all of these opposing representations were presented as confirmed by documents, statistics, memories, and private histories of the inhabitants, Nowa Huta appears in the mass media as a contested city.[4]

The contradictions between the representations of Nowa Huta, all of which were inherited from the communist period, were not new. What was changed after the political transition were the ways these contradictions were dealt with. Before 1989, the method used to tame the contradictions was a scheme of evolution (the narration on the transformation from peasants to workers) or a version of Marxist dialectics, according to which the peasants changed the material conditions of their life by taking up the work in the steelworks and thus are able to overcome the contradiction between the city and the countryside by creating a new socialist society.[5] After the end of communism in Poland both schemes became obsolete. As noticed by Meštrović in his book *The Balkanization of the West: The Confluence of Postmodernism and Postcommunism*: 'communism seems to have collapsed at nearly the same time that postmodernism asserted itself in intellectual discourse' (Meštrović 1994, 2).[6] Thus, the abolition of orthodox Marxism as the official ideology coincided with the postmodern distrust towards all *grands recits* [grand narratives], while the simultaneity of arguments supporting both contradictory theses undermined the credibility of the evolutionary scheme. Deprived of a theory that would allow subsuming the contradictions into a single argument, the commentators accept the impossibility of interrelating the representations of Nowa Huta and frame it as a 'city

---

4   On the representations of space in Nowa Huta, see Stanek 2005.
5   Such arguments can be found, for example, in the article by Wereksiej 1975.
6   On the relationship between postmodernism and postsocialism in art, see Erjavec 2003.

of paradoxes'. This suspends the discussion about the city by reducing its descriptions to a collection of contradictory, yet equally justifiable representations. Moreover, this limbo is often treated as a symptom of the general failure of Nowa Huta as a city. For example, Jerzy Surdykowski, one of the participants of the discussion on Nowa Huta organized shortly after the political change in 1989, claimed:

> Nowa Huta is for me a city of paradoxes. […] I think that Nowa Huta and its paradoxes is a strong argument against programming the future in the name of any intellectual idea, despite the fact that these ideas might be considered today, here and now, correct. (Głos Nowej Huty 1989, 7; translation by the author)[7]

This impasse is rather characteristic for contemporary cities, and a short internet search with Google shows that few contemporary metropolises were not called 'cities of paradoxes'. Thomas Bender wrote recently in the Harvard Design Magazine that 'our capacity to describe or theorize the social and spatial organization of the contemporary metropolis is inadequate to the metropolitan experience' (Bender 2001, 70). The inability of gathering times and spaces in one coherent experience is considered one of the symptoms of the changed conditions of the spatial and temporal practice of late capitalism which has been subsumed by Harvey and Jameson[8] under the broader concept of the crisis of representation. Harvey and Jameson have stressed the importance of technology in triggering this crisis, mainly by new transportation systems (investments in space) and new financial instruments (investments in time) but also mass media, which are important agents in this changed spatio-temporal practice. In this situation, many authors claim, that 'cities have become impossible to describe' (Ingersoll 1992, 5) and even that the effort to "understand or construct a whole" of the 'destabilized, obscure, baseless, mystified' modern city is 'part of a mystification' (Steven Marcus, in Allen 2000, 36, 7).[9]

Simulation in Nowa Huta

Parallel to the impasse in negotiating between contradictory representations of Nowa Huta, one can recognize a tendency to simulation as a means of representing the city, exhibited in even the most diverse social practices. This parallelism seems not to be

---

7   This is a characteristic claim, presenting (in analogy to the logical tradition of the *reductio ad absurdum* [reduction to the absurd]) the paradoxes of Nowa Huta as a proof of the failure of a particular way of planning a city. However, the concept of Nowa Huta as a 'city of paradoxes' is endowed with more nuanced evaluations by other authors (see Gazeta Krakowska 1996 and Stenning 2001, 10).

8   See Harvey 1990, 260ff; Jameson 1984.

9   This situation has a significant consequence for the discipline of architecture: if the city cannot be represented adequately, and the architects are producers of representations of the city, the crisis of representation is perceived as a major threat for the practice of architecture; thus, a significant part of the architectural discussion concerns new possibilities for representation of the contemporary city (see Allen 2000, 36, 174).

accidental: at first glance, simulation is a radical, but understandable answer to the crisis of representation in Nowa Huta. If none of the generalizations concerning this city is adequate, if every representation aiming at extracting some essential features of a city can be opposed by a contradictory one, and both can be supported by historical expertise and personal experiences,[10] then simulation, based on a refusal of any interpretation, generalization or commentary (which in Nowa Huta would be necessarily partial), as a mere repetition of what has been there, seems to be a justified strategy of representation.

There is a series of initiatives and events in Nowa Huta which were based on the principle of simulation and enthusiastically welcomed by both the cultural and political establishment and by publicity-oriented commercial firms. The most symptomatic of them was the exhibition SocLand (2001), organized by the SocLand Foundation, set up by the prominent architect Czesław Bielecki, the celebrated cabaret artist Jacek Fedorowicz and the Oscar-winning director Andrzej Wajda. In the statute of the foundation the organizers write that 'the script and the exhibition, by making use of all media techniques, allows the visitors to experience their lots in life and situations which will show the picture of dangers and misfortunes of man under communism'.[11] Following this statement, the aim of the exhibition was to reconstruct 'one day in communist Poland'; not only were everyday items from that period gathered, but also actors were employed to enact the roles associated with 'communist Poland'. The visitors were acting as well, forced to imitate the everyday situations from that period of time, for example queuing for sausages which were available not for money, but for coupons distributed by Krystyna Zachwatowicz, a prominent stage designer from Kraków and one of the organizers. She explained in an interview that the exhibition was meant to be 'a show, a kind of Disneyland, a several-hour journey through the time of socialism, with party executives, a tribune for speeches and an empty counter with a dried up cheese and a note: "I will be right back"'.[12] The planned follow-up of the exhibition (which is currently being built in the Palace of Culture and Science in Warsaw) develops the idea tested in Nowa Huta, explained by Marek Kozicki, the head of the SocLand Foundation, in the following way:

> The exhibition should express the situation and atmosphere of the time under discussion in possibly emotional and at the same time realistic way. An important part of the exhibition is the 'socialist labyrinth' which will lead the visitor through spaces and situations typical for the real-existing socialism. It will have a character of a ghost-train which you cannot just get on and off. The compulsory visiting of all stations will create the necessary tension and at the same time will reconstruct the atmosphere and the core elements of the world of the real-existing communism in which an average citizen was living. (Kozicki 2005, 143; translation by the author)

---

10   Baudrillard observed that simulation enters the scene where oppositions coexist and implies, that many contradictory representations are true (see Baudrillard 1983, 32).

11   See *Fundacja Socland – Muzeum Komunizmu. Statut.*

12   *Dziennik Polski* 2001, 1, 4. See also *Gazeta w Krakowie/Gazeta Wyborcza* 2001, 7.

In its emotional character and attempt to make the visitors participate in the experiences of the people living in communism, SocLand resembles the museums and exhibitions which were founded in many Central and Eastern European cites after 1989. The contributors to the book *Der Kommunismus im Museum* [Communism in the Museum], which compares the museums and exhibitions about communism in Prague, Tallinn, Riga, Vilnius, Warsaw, Budapest, and Sighet, stress that 'the creation of emotionality and real concerns is often the main aim in the reflection on the communist past' (Knigge and Mählert 2005, 209). This aim is usually achieved by locating the museums in places directly connected to communist terror, often in a prison used by the secret police, like in Vilnius, Budapest, and Sighet and by reconstructing particularly traumatic situations, such as prisoner's barracks (Riga), and the execution path (Vilunius). But in the SocLand exhibition, launched almost ten years ago, one can detect a shift in the focus:

> [The museum] should show the mechanisms of violence and acts of resistance, the shaping of consciousness by means of propaganda, and the persistence in opposition, but first at all it should reveal the most common experience, shared by everybody – the shoddiness, greyness, dependence, competition for trashy goods, prizes and punishments, a constant and simultaneous care and control.[13]

This shift in attention from heroic and traumatic events to the persistent experience of the communist everyday life – both horrifying and grotesque – is what allowed framing the exhibition as a 'Disneyland', as Zachwatowicz put it: an entertaining theme park with some chilling moments.

Figure 9.1 SocLand exhibition in Nowa Huta 2001
Source: Fundacja Socland, Muzeum Komunizmu.

---

13 *Fundacja Socland – Muzeum Komunizmu. Misja*; translation by the author.

Figure 9.2 SocLand exhibition in Nowa Huta 2001
Source: Fundacja Socland, Muzeum Komunizmu.

Simulation in Nowa Huta, however, was not restricted to the SocLand exhibition. A similar principle of a repetition of an activity from the past was the founding idea of a project of Nowa Huta's museum, discussed in the local press in 1999: a sea of mud in which the visitors could paddle in rubber boots was conceived as the highlight of the envisioned exhibition. This refers to the mythical mud in Nowa Huta, present in all contemporary reports about the building site. Another planned attraction was a reconstructed dwelling from the 1950s and 1960s with a trough for a pig kept by the first inhabitants in the block of flats.[14] One advertising agency suggested a promotion campaign for the city relying on a restoration of the old part of Nowa Huta to the character of the 1950s, with the cars from this time, neon signs and original furnishing of the bars.[15] Such a way of thinking was supported by prominent members of Kraków's establishment. Zygmunt Kruczek (from the Institute of Tourism at the Kraków's Academy of Physical Education) claimed that an 'open-air museum is a great idea […], foreign tourists would be delighted'[16] and Jacek Purchla (head of the Department of Urban Studies in Institute of Art History at the Jagiellonian University and the director of the International Cultural Center in Kraków) said that Nowa Huta was 'a ready made […] theme-park, whose

---

14   The idea of the museum was explained by Maciej Miezian, an cultural activist and author of the tourist guide about Nowa Huta; see *Magazyn and Rzeczpospolita* 1999.

15   See *Gazeta w Krakowie/Gazeta Wyborcza* 2000a.

16   *Gazeta w Krakowie/Gazeta Wyborcza* 2000b.

attractiveness should be used for tourist reasons'.[17] One realized attempt at a scenario based on simulation was an action of the RMF, a commercial radio network from Kraków, which instigated a provocative event in the center of Nowa Huta in the very place where before 1989 the Lenin monument was standing. On the morning of 22 July 2001[18] a foam life-size copy of the Lenin statue was positioned on the pedestal of the former monument.[19] In an interview, the organizer admitted that the aim was to 'probe how the people will react on the reappearance of Lenin and whether a come-back to communism would be possible'.[20]

Figure 9.3 The foam copy of the Lenin monument in the Aleja Róz in Nowa Huta

Source: Anna Kaczmarz, Dziennik Polski.

Even if the event was not much more than a publicity-oriented provocation, this statement reveals the typically ambiguous mixture of political and tourist aims of almost all mentioned exhibitions and proposals. However, parallel to this ambiguity these events introduce a sharp distinction between the visitors – the target customers – and the inhabitants. This division is one of the most characteristic effects of urban simulations, as some of the authors of an influential book *Variations on the Theme*

---

17   See *Gazeta Krakowska* 1996.

18   Under communism, 22 July was the most important national holiday (the Day of the Rebirth of Poland).

19   *See Głos Tygodnik Nowohucki* 2001.

20   *Dziennik Polski/Kronika Krakowska 2001a.*

Park (Sorkin 1992) have shown.[21] By addressing the visitors to Nowa Huta as the target group of the simulations, and choosing the grotesque and horrifying everyday as symptomatic for the communist experience, the events created a clear-cut division between the roles offered to the visitors and those imposed to the residents: if the visitor could choose between perceiving herself as a tourist, an historian, or a political commentator, the inhabitant's choice was restricted to the much less attractive role of a victim, collaborator, actor, or living fossil.

Consequently, the unequivocal negative reactions of the inhabitants and local leaders on these ideas should be seen as a rejection of these roles offered to the residents of Nowa Huta. The copy of the Lenin monument was toppled from the pedestal by passers-by and one of the aldermen (a member of LPR, a far-right party) notified the public prosecutor's office about an 'attempt to propagate a totalitarian system',[22] which is a crime in Poland. A local magazine quotes an inhabitant, who complains that 'they want to push us back to communism'.[23] An enthusiastic review of the SocLand exhibition in a Kraków local newspaper ironically mentioned a comment made by an inhabitant who said that 'his wife told him that it is a joke' but 'he does not understand such jokes'. This statement (in a colloquial language, suggesting an uneducated speaker) was used as the title of the article, contrasting the enthusiasm of the journalist and the alleged ignorance of the inhabitant.[24] The idea of a restoration of the appearance of the city from the 1950s was decidedly rejected and the local press quotes an accusation of 'a lack of respect for the inhabitants of Nowa Huta' who do not want to be 'apes in the zoo'.[25]

Those unanimously critical reactions – susceptible to political manipulations and commented on in a patronizing way by some journalists – are worthy of attention. Particularly, when we keep in mind the fact that Nowa Huta is a contested place, and that even among the inhabitants there is no consensus concerning the representations of the city. This may indicate that the protests of the inhabitants who do not recognize themselves and their city in the simulations are directed not against a distorted representation (which could be corrected) or an ideology (which might be replaced by an accurate effigy), but rather against a simulation as a mode of representation. This could be supported by a comment made by Jean Baudrillard, who recognized that simulation is destructive to its referent. In *The Precession of Simulacra* Baudrillard writes that 'the age of simulation [...] begins with a liquidation of all referentials'

---

21   For example, describing lower Manhattan's South Street Seaport, an example of instrumental simulation of the urban history very different to Nowa Huta, Christine Boyer points out that the target customers were not the inhabitants, but the well-off visitors: 'most of the contemporary enclaves along New York's once-forgotten waterfront are postindustrial service centers planned to attract the young urban professionals and double-income childless couples increasingly populating the city'. (1992, 184)

22   *Dziennik Polski/Kronika Krakowska* 2001b, see also *Dziennik Polski/Kronika Krakowska* 2001c.

23   *Głos Tygodnik Nowohucki* 2001.

24   See *Gazeta w Krakowie/Gazeta Wyborcza* 2001.

25   *Gazeta w Krakowie/Gazeta Wyborcza* 2000a.

(Baudrillard 1983, 4). It is, however, his analysis of Disneyland which might be most helpful to understand what happens in Nowa Huta:

> Disneyland is there to conceal the fact that it is the 'real' country, all of 'real' America, which *is* Disneyland (just as prisons are there to conceal the fact that it is the social in its entirety, in its banal omnipresence, which is carceral). Disneyland is presented as imaginary in order to make us believe that the rest is real, when in fact all of Los Angeles and the America surrounding it are no longer real, but of the order of the hyperreal and of simulation. It is no longer a question of a false representation of reality (ideology), but of concealing the fact that the real is no longer real, and thus of saving the reality principle. (Baudrillard 1983, 25)

An analogous mechanism seems to be working in Nowa Huta: the effort to simulate the communist everyday life suggests, that without this effort the relicts of communism in Poland would deteriorate and the memories would fade ('the older of us want to forget [communism] and for the younger the absurdity of this time is something not real' – write the organizers of the SocLand exhibition).[26] Thus, the ostentatiously communist Nowa Huta reduced to a harmless fake is less a deterrent than a proof, that the country has nothing to do with communism any more. The triumphalist tone of the organizers of the SocLand exhibition, all prominent members of the Polish cultural establishment, indicates, that this was precisely the aim of the exhibition: to celebrate the ultimate end of communism in Poland, shown as an ethnological curiosity, at the expense of Nowa Huta and its inhabitants.

In the local press of Nowa Huta one can often find the suggestion that the inadequacy of the representations of Nowa Huta stems from the fact that they are produced by visitors for visitors, and not by inhabitants for inhabitants. Interestingly, the already quoted remark about the inhabitants who 'do not want to be apes in the zoo' reappeared some years later, when the inhabitants, asked for an opinion about a recent film festival in Nowa Huta, were reported to say that 'films about us always resemble pictures from a zoo'.[27] Consequently, as a remedy it was proposed to close the gap between representation in the sense of 'effigy' and representation in the sense of 'deputation' by including the representatives of the inhabitants in the processes of the production of representations of Nowa Huta.[28] But locating the reason of the problem in the fact that the majority of the representations were produced externally would be misleading. What can be learned from the discussed examples is that any kind of participation which takes place within the mode of simulation, even a struggle against simulation, subjugates the participants to the simulation. This was revealed when the passers-by knocked off the foam copy of the

---

26   *Fundacja Socland – Muzeum Komunizmu. Misja.*

27   *Gazeta w Krakowie/Gazeta Wyborcza* 2002.

28   Many authors stress the interdependence between these two meanings of 'representation', most strongly Thomas Bender, who argues that 'visual representation and deliberative (or formal political) representation are complementary aspects of a democratic public'. (Bender 2001, 73)

Lenin monument, thus becoming a part of the simulation by repeating the gestures – automatic and meaningless – of the demonstrators who attacked the original monument in December 1989. Even the photography shown in Figure 9.3, published in the daily *Dziennik Polski*, supports the simulation: it shows the children looking to the camera from behind the crashed monument like a group of revolutionaries who have just profaned the symbol of the *ancien régime* [old order].[29]

Simulation, which operates with images, objects, and practices, turned into fetishes of consumption and political signs, petrifies the subversive potentials of urban space; Lefebvre was aware of this danger, when he was writing in *La Révolution Urbaine* [The Urban Revolution]:

> We can speak of a *colonization* of the urban space, which takes place in the street through the spectacle of objects – a 'system of objects' that has become symbol and spectacle. [...] The parades, masquerades, balls, and folklore festivals authorized by a power structure caricaturize the appropriation and reappropriation of space. (Lefebvre 1970, 32–33; translation Lefebvre 2003, 21)

This may suggest that the spontaneous protests of the inhabitants were not directed against an insufficient or distorted representation, but (perhaps intuitively) against the conditions of this representation – namely simulation – imposed on them by the dominant (cultural, political, economic) practices. Thus, instead of regarding participation as a general solution for the representation, what must be looked for is an alternative mode of representation in which participation would make the difference.

The asymptotic mode of representation

Contrary to the claims of Baudrillard that simulation 'bears no relation to any reality whatsoever' (1983, 12), the simulations in Nowa Huta were applied as a general framework which allowed gathering images, objects, emotions, memories, people, and practices, by this sustaining heterogeneous and miscellaneous relations to urban reality. Thus, recognizing simulation not as an inevitable result of the historical development, described by Baudrillard as the 'fourth phase of the image' (1983, 11), but as selectively mobilized by specialized practices (politics, tourism, institutionalized education, entertainment) allows looking for alternative models for representing Nowa Huta. I would like to search for such models in the performance *Nowa Huta – doświadczenie* [Nowa Huta – the experience] by the French director Bruno Lajara, and in a project by Nowa Łaźnia *Mieszkam tu* [I live here]. These projects suggest an alternative to simulation not because they provide a more faithful image of Nowa Huta, but because they reorganize and destabilize the roles assigned to the producers and receivers of representations.

---

29 A famous example of such a photograph is one from the Gernsheim Collection (University of Texas, Austin), which shows the Communards standing behind the statue of Napoleon I from the Vendôme Column, toppled in May 1871.

The spectacle, presented during the *baz@rt* theater festival in Kraków (2004), was subtitled *Co się wydarzyło w Nowej Hucie?* [What happened in Nowa Huta?] and featured both professional actors and the inhabitants of the city. The performance consisted almost only of quotations and images of Nowa Huta, and yet its general theme was precisely the distance between Nowa Huta and its representation. In order to present how this theme was dealt with, I would like to describe some particular scenes of the performance.

One of the scenes, in which the distance between Nowa Huta and its representation could be experienced, was staged in the courtyard behind the theater. The actor was delivering a monologue: in vulgar language he explained in a wordy way his ideas of a happy life. Due to sudden jumps between the plots and the triteness of his opinions, the declamation sounded like a stereotyped imitation. When the actor left, an interview with an unemployed young inhabitant of Nowa Huta was screened; it was he who was the author of the text said by the actor: the sudden changes in the themes reflected the questions of the interviewer (which were left out in the performance of the actor). Through repetition, the text did not gain more authenticity; on the contrary – it deprived the interviewee of immediacy, actually made him sound fake.[30] A similar procedure was applied in other scenes, when we – the spectators – were forced to simulate fear (of the threats of an actor) or interest (for a story told by an older inhabitant of Nowa Huta who offered us orange juice in a room furnished as a typical flat in this city). As Baudrillard noticed about the Lascaux caves, 'the duplication is sufficient to render both [i.e. the original and its copy] artificial' (1983, 18). A similar mechanism could be experienced in the described scenes: in spite of the direct or mediated participation of the inhabitants of Nowa Huta, these scenes evoked a feeling of the foreignness of the city rather than a sense of familiarity.

Figure 9.4 'Nowa Huta – the experience', directed by Bruno Lajara 2004
Source: Ryszard Kornecki, Teatr Stary w Krakowie.

---

30   Importantly, the actor did not see this video before the performance, see the interview with the director in *Gazeta w Krakowie/Gazeta Wyborcza* 2004.

This experience of distance between Nowa Huta and its simulation, in order to be consciously noticed, requires a shift in the position of the spectator who becomes an observer of his own feelings or an onlooker from Kraków, who tries to understand the distant Nowa Huta. Yet this comfortable position was untenable during the performance. In the last scene, for example, a video was screened, showing older inhabitants recalling the everyday problems of the first years of the city, personal situations, political riots. As spectators (mostly young people), we were assigned to a role of the onlookers of these confessions. At the end of every interview, the filmed person sang a song chosen by her (at the request of the director, who does not speak Polish). Owing to the song – usually from the youth of the filmed person – her story did not gain more content, but more autonomy; because of the form less transparent for the bystander than the everyday language, the story itself became less transparent. Raising our heads and looking at the mezzanine, we began to realize that we were deprived of our position of observers – we have noticed, that we ourselves were observed by the members of the choir of Nowa Huta, consisting chiefly of the people shown in the video. The initial division between the observed and observers was inverted. Similarly in other scenes; when a video on the everyday activities of an older inhabitant of Nowa Huta was accompanied by an aria, the spectator recognized the contrast as an aesthetic convention. Yet this position collapsed when the featured person appeared in a red dress and offered to sing the previously played aria. This is also how the spectacle ended: when the choir sang a Nowa Huta hit from the 1950s, the spectator ceased to be an observer by becoming a guest – foreign and polite.

Figure 9.5 'Nowa Huta – the experience', directed by Bruno Lajara 2004
Source: Ryszard Kornecki, Teatr Stary w Krakowie.

The described performance consisted of a series of well-directed situations, in which the spectator experienced the dynamics between the foreignness and closeness of Nowa Huta, its strangeness and familiarity, without losing the feeling of staying in touch with the city. Unlike in Brecht's *Verfremdung* [Estrangement],[31] the spectator does not question the stability of the character, but is compelled to challenge her own stability, being forced to switch between the roles of an objective observer, curious tourist, indifferent bystander, polite guest. All of these roles introduced another convention which became the framework of representation – for example, the change from the position of an observer to a position of a guest means a change of the conventional criteria of objectivity for the conventional criteria of politeness. The way of engagement in the representation is constructed by the producer of representation, but it is the spectator who decides whether to accept and apply the suggested convention, or to reject it; it is possible, for example, to regard the inhabitant of Nowa Huta who tells the story about her youth as an actress, but in a certain moment it becomes obviously impolite – perhaps one should recognize politeness and hospitality as epistemic categories. At the same time, the position of the inhabitants is also destabilized, exploring the ambiguity between being an inhabitant and playing an inhabitant.

It is not by chance, that Łaźnia Nowa, an influential cultural center which relocated from Kazimierz, the Jewish District in Kraków, to Nowa Huta in 2004, was referred to as 'labyrinth of hospitality'.[32] The adequacy of this name is particularly evident in the project *Mieszkam tu*, organized in 2004 and 2005 as a part of the festival *Genius Loci w Nowej Hucie*. The Figure 9.6 shows that the organizers managed to transform the abandoned workshops of the electric secondary school (which educated workers for the Steelworks) into a hospitable and atmospheric environment. The participants of this project – the inhabitants of Nowa Huta – were asked to donate objects which were significant and valuable for them as gifts for the invited artists and writers.[33] These objects – a signaling lamp, a guitar, an emblem of the Solidarność trade union – were described by the inhabitants and reappeared in the short stories and drama pieces published in one book and transformed into a piece played in Łaźnia Nowa (May 2005), directed by Jacek Papis.[34] These texts programmatically hovered

---

31 Brecht explained his strategy of *Verfremdung* in the following way: 'the spectator will no longer see the people on stage shown as unalterable, uninfluencable, helplessly delivered over to their fate. He will see that this man is such and such, because circumstances are such. And circumstances are such and such, because man is such. But he is conceivable not only as he is now, but also otherwise – as he might be – and the circumstances as well are conceivable as being different than they are.' (Brecht 1967, 302. translation by the author)

32 Lodołamacz 2005a.

33 The artists invited were: Jacek Papis, Paweł Jurek, Paweł Sala, Radosław Dobrowolski, Małgorzata Owsiany, Sławek Shuty, Mariusz Sienkiewicz. The texts were published by Łaźnia Nowa in a booklet.

34 Comp. Lodołamacz 2005b, 2005c, 2005d.

between the stories of the inhabitants related to the objects and the experience of temporary 'inhabiting' of Nowa Huta by the artists themselves.[35]

Figure 9.6 'I lived here', spectacle in Łaźnia Nowa 2004
Source: Krescenty Głazik.

The way Nowa Huta is represented in both projects may be considered as reacting to the crisis of representation in Nowa Huta in a way that is very different to the previously discussed simulation: instead of accepting the inability of gathering inconsistent representations into one stable whole, one accepts the necessary instability of this whole. In analogy to the way of writing of Henri Lefebvre, one can call this way of representing urban reality 'asymptotical'. Lefebvre described his work in the following way:

> For such a cognition as ours, which starting from the 'real' proceeds via the categories and the application of the already worked out concepts, although the 'reality' is neither inaccessible nor transcendent, it is set as an (asymptotical) border in the infinite for the finite cognition. (1977, 141. translation by the author)

In his writings Lefebvre regarded concepts as 'asymptotical borders' of reality and applied them in order to define a particular argument as a series of shifts in-

---

35 In recent years one can observe some other projects in Nowa Huta which focus on participation and can be seen as relating representation with hospitality: the project *nowa-huta.rtf* (see Anon. 2005/2006), the project *Nowa Sztuka w Nowej Hucie* (see Anon. 2004), and the project *Feniks* (see Miodyńska and Walter 2004).

Encountering Urban Places

between these concepts. Similarly, asymptotical representation is understood as a constant process of shifting between various types of contact with the city and its inhabitants. If the simulation framed the visitors and the inhabitants with a set of confronting roles founded on fixed economic or historical oppositions (tourist and actors, political activists and victims or collaborators of the regime), the asymptotic mode of representation destabilized those positions by introducing a plurality of transitive roles, like the role of the guest, which leave space for real interaction. Hospitality involves invitation, which was the foundation of both spectacles: the invited inhabitants were inviting visitors. Thus, participation of the inhabitants in the creation of representation and their hospitality is a defining moment of asymptotical representation. This process – a practice itself – has a potential to be designed as interrelated with other urban practices, and marked by discussions, articles, projects and, finally, buildings and urban spaces.[36]

References

Allen, S. (2000), *Practice: Architecture, Technique and Representation* (London: Routledge).

Anon. (2004), *Nowa Sztuka w Nowej Hucie/New Art in Nowa Huta* (Kraków: MIK).

Anon. (2005/2006), *Temat na Willowym,* nine leaflets (Kraków: MIK).

Baudrillard, J. (1983) *Simulations* (New York: Semiotext[e]).

Bender, T. (2001), 'The New Metropolitanism and the Pluralized Public', Harvard Design Magazine, Winter/ Spring, 70.

Boyer, C. (1992), 'Cities for Sale: Merchandising History at South Street Seaport', in Sorkin (ed.).

Brecht, B. (1967), 'Über das experimentelle Theater', in Brecht, B. (1967), Gesammelte Werke, vol. 15 (Frankfurt am Main: Suhrkamp).

Erjavec, A. (ed.) (2003), *Postmodernism and the Postsocialist Condition. Politicized Art under Late Socialism* (Berkeley: University of California Press).

Harvey, D. (1990), *The Condition of Postmodernity: An Enquiry Into the Origins of Cultural Change* (Oxford: Blackwell).

Ingersoll, R. (1992), 'The Disappearing Suburb', Design Book Review 26, Fall, 5.

Jameson, F. (1984), *Postmodernism, or the Cultural Logic of Late Capitalism* (London: Verso).

Knigge, V. and Mählert, U. (eds) (2005), *Der Kommunismus im Museum. Formen der Auseinandersetzung in Deutschland und Ostmitteleuropa* (Köln: Böhlau Verlag).

Kozicki, M. (2005) 'Das Kommunismus-Museum SocLand in Warschau', in Knigge

36 I am very grateful to Christine Boyer (Princeton University), Patrick Healy (Technical University Delft) and Alison Stenning (University of Newcastle) for their careful readings and comments.

and Mählert (eds).
Lefebvre, H. (1970), *La révolution urbaine* (Paris: Gallimard).
Lefebvre, H. (1977), *Kritik des Alltagslebens*, vol. II (Frankfurt am Main: Athäneum).
Lefebvre, H. (1991), *The Production of Space* (Oxford: Blackwell).
Lefebvre, H. (2003), *The Urban Revolution* (Minneapolis: University of Minnesota Press).
Meštrović, S. (1994), *The Balkanization of the West: The Confluence of Postmodernism and Postcommunism* (London: Routledge).
Miodyńska, A. and Walter, A. (eds) (2004), *Feniks. Projekt dla Nowej Huty* (Kraków: MIK).
Puttkamer, J. (2005), 'Die Museen des Kommunismus. Ein Kommentar aus fachwissenschaftlicher Sicht', in Knigge and Mählert (eds).
Sorkin, M. (ed.) (1992), *Variations on a Theme Park. The New American City and the End of Public Space* (New York: Hill and Wang).
Stenning, A. (2005d), 'Beyond Monoindustralism. Rethinking Nowa Huta Beyond the Kombinat' paper presented at the workshop 'The Futurism of Industrial City – 100 years of Wolfsburg/Nowa Huta', Nowa Huta, 10 September 2005.

Articles in newspapers

Dziennik Polski (2001), 'Socjalizm dla wszystkich', *Dziennik Polski*, 156:17342, 1, 4.
Dziennik Polski/Kronika Krakowska (2001a), 'Lenin w prokuraturze', *Dziennik Polski/Kronika Krakowska*, 171:17357, II.
Dziennik Polski/Kronika Krakowska (2001b), 'Zakazane żarty', *Dziennik Polski/Kronika Krakowska*, 172:17358, III.
Dziennik Polski/Kronika Krakowska (2001c), 'Powrócił bez zezwolenia', *Dziennik Polski/Kronika Krakowska*, 170:17356), I.
Gazeta Krakowska (1996), 'Stara Nowa Huta', *Gazeta Krakowska*, 29, 13.
Gazeta w Krakowie/Gazeta Wyborcza (2000a), 'Sprzedać socrealizm', *Gazeta w Krakowie/Gazeta Wyborcza*, 211:3163, 1.
Gazeta w Krakowie/Gazeta Wyborcza (2000b), 'Propozycje na gorąco', *Gazeta w Krakowie/Gazeta Wyborcza*, 211:3163, 2.
Gazeta w Krakowie/Gazeta Wyborcza (2001), 'Żona mówiła, że to jaja', *Gazeta w Krakowie/Gazeta Wyborcza*, 217:3472, 7.
Gazeta w Krakowie/Gazeta Wyborcza (2002), 'Niesamowicie egzotyczne', *Gazeta w Krakowie/Gazeta Wyborcza*, 166, 5.
Głos Nowej Huty (1989), 'Symbol, sukces, porażka?', *Głos Nowej Huty*, 40:1693, 7.
Głos Tygodnik Nowohucki (2001), 'Lenin (na chwilę) wrócił', *Głos Tygodnik*

Nowohucki, 538, 2.

Lodołamacz (2005a), 'Mieszkam tu', *Lodołamacz,* 1:04, 6.

Lodołamacz (2005b), '(Nie) mieszkam tu', *Lodołamacz,* 1:04, 8.

Lodołamacz (2005c), 'Mieszkam tu', *Lodołamacz,* 4,5:07/08, 4.

Lodołamacz (2005d), 'Mieszkam tu', *Lodołamacz,* 2:05, 7.

Magazyn/Rzeczpospolita (1999), 'Była Mogiła', *Magazyn/Rzeczpospolita,* 23, 10–15.

Rzeczpospolita (2002), 'Dzieje wielkiej manipulacji', *Rzeczpospolita,* 241:6318.

Wereksiej, F. (1975), 'Jubileuszowe obrachunki', *WTK Tygodnik Katolicki,* 35, 1, 8.

Internet sources

Brenner, N. (2000), 'The urban question as a scale question: reflections on Henri Lefebvre, urban theory and the politics of scale', *NYU Department of Sociology* [webpage] <http://sociology.fas.nyu.edu/docs/IO/222/2000.Brenner.IJURR.pdf> accessed 6 March 2006.

'Fundacja Socland – Muzeum Komunizmu. Statut.', *SOCLAND - muzeum komunizmu* [webpage] <http://www.socland.pl/textstat.html> accessed 6 March 2006.

'Fundacja Socland – Muzeum Komunizmu. Misja', *SOCLAND - muzeum komunizmu* [webpage] <http://www.socland.pl/main.html> accessed 6 March 2006.

Gazeta w Krakowie/Gazeta Wyborcza (2004) 'Potwór w Zamku Kafki', *Dziennik Teatralny* [webpage] <http://www.teatry.art.pl/!rozmowy/potwori.htm> accessed 6 March 2006.

Stanek, Ł. (2005), 'The production of urban space by mass media storytelling practices: Nowa Huta as a case study', paper presented at the conference 'The Work of Stories', Massachusetts Institute of Technology, 6–8 May 2005, *Massachusetts Institute of Technology* [webpage] <http://web.mit.edu/comm-forum/mit4/papers/stanek.pdf> accessed 6 March 2006.

Stenning, A. (2001), 'Representing Transformations/Transforming Representations: Remaking Life and Work in Nowa Huta, Poland', paper presented to WES 2001: Winning and Losing in the New Economy, University of Nottingham, 11–13 September 2001, *nowahuta.info* [webpage] <http://www.nowahuta.info/papers/ba2002.pdf> accessed 7 March 2006.

Stenning, A. (2003), 'Shaping the economic landscapes of post-socialism? Labour, workplace and community in Nowa Huta, Poland', *nowahuta.info* [webpage] <http://www.nowahuta.info/publications/stenning_antipode.pdf> accessed 7 March 2006.

Stenning, A. (2005a), 'Re-placing work: Economic transformations and the shape of a community in post-socialist Poland', *nowahuta.info* [webpage] <http://www.nowahuta.info/papers/stenning%20wes%20formatted.pdf> accessed 7 March 2006.

Stenning, A. (2005b), 'The transformation of life, work and community in post-socialist Europe: A westerner studies Nowa Huta', *nowahuta.info* [webpage]

<http://www.nowahuta.info/papers/Stenning%20Geog%20Pol.pdf> accessed 7 March 2006.

Stenning, A. (2005c), 'Where is the post-socialist working class? Working class lives in the spaces of (post-)socialism', *nowahuta.info* [webpage] <http://www.nowahuta.info/papers/postsocialist%20working%20class%20revised%20final.pdf> accessed 7 March 2006.

Chapter 10

Sensing Place – Mobile and Wireless Technologies in Urban Space

Katharine S. Willis

Introduction

One of the primary ways we perceive the world is spatial; the physical form and appearance of our environment is fundamental to our actions and perceptions within it. However, in an increasingly mobile society with ubiquitous access to communication technologies, perceptions of space are transformed. In order to understand the consequences of this transformation it is important to first investigate the nature of our experience of space.

Through particular encounters or experiences perceptual space is differentiated into places, or sites of specific meaning or intention. These places can be created by everyday practice, such as the significance of a particular street corner on a route walked daily, or can be more ephemeral, such as a striking view once seen during a trip abroad that has endured as a memory. The experience of place manifests itself as an identification with the setting, which is referred to as a 'sense of place'. This attribute of place is not just a perceptual response to a physical location, but also the result of an ordering and categorization of our spatial experience. As such, places reside not only in reality but also in abstract mental conceptions, which are a combination of commonly perceived and highly personalized images. These mental images of space enable us to weave together multiple, fragmented experiences into more coherent and manageable concepts, which then guide our subsequent action and perception in space. Yet we are increasingly confronted with environments that are offering new mediated forms of action and perception in space, facilitated by communications technologies. A key feature of such technologies is that they are both mobile and wireless and as such they transcend existing physical notions of space and place. In attempting to un-weave the experience of space in the increasingly mediated environments there is a need to reconsider the frameworks in which we interact and communicate in spatial settings.

In our everyday experience, cities exist as concentrated sites of encounter and interaction, but curiously communication is often not treated as part of the everyday infrastructure of urban life. This arises out of the simple fact that communications technologies are both literally and metaphorically invisible. Since cities are traditionally conceived primarily in terms of physical form and visual experience, this brings into question how we can form adequate modes of understanding and representing our interactions in urban settings. As mobile and wireless technologies proliferate in urban space, they can be considered as having an existence in terms of several spaces, those of places that make up our everyday direct experience and those of the digital nodes and networks that facilitate communication. When these virtually invisible and immaterial mediated layers are overlaid and integrated within urban space, it alters both the space and the ways that people act within it. In order to investigate these emerging experiences more intricately some sites of communication technologies in the city will be studied in a specific urban setting, and conclusions drawn about the implications for the resultant spatial experience.

Place and space

Our experience of our spatial surroundings is both dynamic and multi-faceted, and as such requires that we constantly employ methods for both recognizing and ordering that which is perceived. One of the key ways in which we order our experience of the spatial world is to ascribe meaning to the static physical setting, enabling highly individual interpretations and actions. In this manner, the individual cannot be seen as entirely distinct from the space in which they find themselves; instead, their presence and action may be seen as inextricably entwined with that setting. This experience is often used to describe the nature of an attribute described as 'place', where particular encounters and experiences are richly differentiated into places, or centers of personal significance (Relph 1976, 11). Perceptual space is differentiated into places or centers of special personal significance through particular encounters and experiences. This process may be abstract and highly personalized but a common characteristic is that this experience is understood as having physical form, and visual appearance (Relph 1976, 30). Whilst places are considered as located, the mere condition of location and position is neither necessary nor a sufficient condition of place. In our everyday lives we do not experience places as distinct, clearly defined entities that can be described simply in terms of their location and appearance. Instead places occur at all levels of identity, scale and meaning: my home, the street corner, the public square, a city, even a continent, but one commonality is that places never allow simple categorization. They all overlap and assimilate with one another and are open to a variety of interpretations.

The organization of thinking, perception, and meaning is intimately related to specific places. The subjective experience of place is highlighted by the perception of whether it is experienced as an insider or outsider. As an insider, being inside is experienced as knowing where you are, where one is surrounded by a place and is part of it. These zones of belonging or identifying with a place are intensified by our intention, and therefore as our intentions vary, so the boundary between inside and outside moves or transforms. The threshold between inside and outside creates not only a boundary condition, but also the possibility of transition, a passage from insider to outsider. The experience of being an insider is characterized as a spatial identification with our surroundings manifested as a 'sense of place'. It is this quality of space, which is often difficult to define in precise terms, that perhaps best exemplifies both the richness of our spatial experience and also how it informs our actions and perceptions in the world.

Space and identity

In order for the perception of space to be meaningful there is a need for spatial identification with our surroundings, which is most directly manifested as an awareness of this feeling of a 'sense of place'. Identity is the basic feature of our experience of places, and both influences and is influenced by those experiences. Indeed, the forming of identity is fundamentally a situated process; perceptions of self, identity, and memory are inextricably linked with our sense of belonging in a spatial setting. As such identity is in part a quality that exists outside of a specific time, but is a result of experience. The identity of place is a distinctiveness that persists despite changes in physical form or appearance. This refers not only to the distinctiveness of individual places, but also to the sameness with different places (Relph 1976, 44).

A further way in which identity of a place is understood is as a mental image or picture, a visual representation in the mind of the individual. We interpret perceptual experience of space into internal representations. The image of a place consists of all the elements associated with the experiences of individuals or groups and their intentions towards that place. Lynch established the concept of environmental image or cognitive maps of urban space (Lynch 1960, 4), and stated that for a city to be more fully experienced the imageability or intelligible elements of the city needs to be understood. An imageable place is one that that can be comprehended over time as a pattern of high continuity with many distinctive parts clearly connected (Lynch 1960, 9). Indeed for most purposes the image of a place is its identity and to understand something of the content and structure of images is an essential prerequisite for understanding identity. This process of image construction is also referred to as cognitive mapping, and is a process composed of a series of psychological transformations by which an individual acquires, codes, recalls, and decodes information about relative locations and attributes in a spatial environment (Downs and Stea 1973, 9). The parallel process of identity construction appears to consist of a complex and gradual ordering and evaluation of observations and expectations, *a priori* ideas with direct experiences, until a stable image is developed. In terms of the spatial setting this is manifest only when the place is plausible enough for the individual to be able to assimilate an enduring mental image.

Mediated space

The essentially physical view of space has always deeply influenced all forms
of spatial analysis. We identify with space as having visual appearance and
physical form, whether this exists in the perceptual present or cognitively as a
representation. However as our experience of the world is increasingly mediated
by communications technologies our relation to place and to place-bound identities
becomes fundamentally changed (Carter *et al.* 1993, 323). One critical characteristic
of these technologies is that the technology itself ceases to be the focus of the activity
and instead vanishes into the background so that the focus is instead on the activity
itself and the environment in which it is occurring; a form of computing referred
to as 'ubiquitous'. The emergence of such ubiquitous technologies has enabled
communications technologies to escape from the traditional physical confines of
built space, since they can be both embedded and mobile. Consequently ubiquitous
computers reside in the human world and they weave themselves into the fabric of
everyday life (Weiser 1994, 94).

Mobile and wireless technologies are a form of ubiquitous computing that create
numerous opportunities for communicating in multiple and varied locations without
the requirement for a wired connection. Such technologies include mobile telephones
and portable PDAs,[1] short-range transmission technologies such as Bluetooth[2] and
RFID,[3] positioning information delivered via satellite to GPS[4] devices, and last but
by no means least WiFi[5] enabling wireless internet access. All of these have been
proliferating and have over the last decade become common means of enabling
communication. As such technologies move out of structured and enclosed physical
environments, their interaction with the physical world reconfigures established
structures of spatial identification in physical environments. Simply put, physically
bounded spaces are less significant when information is able to pass through walls and
simultaneously travel great distances. As a result, where one is has less and less to do
with what one knows and experiences. (Meyrowitz 1986, viii). But communication
technologies are inherently spatial, in that they enable communication at a distance,
and as such free communication from a fixed location in urban space. On the one
hand such communications technologies, which whilst crucial in supporting the
mobility and flux, are also fixed networks that must be embedded in space. But they
also consist of physical systems made up of links and nodes that are constructed
fundamentally of spatial systems linking together places (Hepworth 1987, quoted
in Graham and Marvin 1996, 50). The media theorist Castells has popularized this
space as the 'space of flows'; a concept where space is understood as linking up
electronically separate locations in an interactive network that connects activities
and people in distinct geographical contexts. He contrasts this with the concept of the

---

1   PDA is an abbreviation for 'Personal Digital Assistant'.
2   Bluetooth is a reference to digital transmission on short range radio frequencies.
3   RFID is an abbreviation for 'Radio Frequency Identification'.
4   GPS is an abbreviation for 'Global Positioning System'.
5   WiFi is a wireless local area network.

'space of places', which he defines as organizing experiences and activity around the confines of locality. The complexity of the urban condition arises when the emerging space of flows is folded into the space of places (Castells 2004, 86).

Similarly, the view of space as some sort of container, which bounds perception and action, no longer provides an adequate description for the spatial manifestation of media technologies. Instead, a more complex framework is necessary, where multiple spaces and times become overlaid within the framework of a single experience such that places are no longer defined by their physical boundaries. Physical boundaries still exist but only to the extent that possibility exists for access to information to be restricted by physical access.

Situations and encounters

In common with the proliferation of communications technologies, increased physical mobility has had a similar transformative effect on perception and behavior in spatial settings. In fact, the two conditions are fundamentally linked, since before electronic telecommunications, when all communication necessitated physical movement, action over distance was only possible through physical movement (Graham and Marvin 1996, 114). Movement from situation to situation involved movement from place to place. However, information input and output has replaced modes of transit usually associated with the movement of people or objects traditionally distributed in space (Virilio 1997, 56). When we communicate through new media, where we are physically no longer determines where we are socially. The twin potentials of mobility and communication have undermined the traditional relationship between physical setting and social situation. Walls, doors, gates, and distances still frame and isolate encounters, but communications media increasingly trespass on the situations that take place in physically defined settings. They re-organize the social settings in which people interact, weakening the once strong relationship between physical place and social place (Meyrowitz 1986, ix). Physical presence is no longer a significant factor in the experiences of people and events, since it is both a possibility and a routine to communicate directly with others without meeting in the same physical place. Consequently, the physical frameworks that once created distinct spatial settings for interaction have been greatly diminished in social significance. Communications technologies have further social implications, in that they enable individuals to escape from place-defined groups and conversely permit outsiders to invade unfamiliar group territories without even entering them.

It is not the physical setting itself that determines the nature of the interaction, but the patterns of social information flow. Places are the settings in which people interact, and as such space, frames human action and also importantly behavior. In fact, spaces are turned into places when social interactions occur. In order for these places to be meaningful they must work on two levels: they must be present an imageable configuration of physical space, which is complimented by a plausible conception of how social interactions can take place in it. As such, spaces become understood as places when they become settings for encounters and situations.

However, to include mediated encounters in the study of situations there is a need to move away from the notion that social situations are only encounters that occur face to face in set times and places (Meyrowitz, 1986, 36–37). The boundaries around social situations affect behavior not only because they often fully include or exclude participants. Communications media affect the definition of situations by bypassing traditional physical restrictions on information flow. By changing the boundaries of social situations, communications media do not simply give us quicker or more thorough access to events and behaviors. They give us instead new events and new behaviors (Carter *et al*. 1993, 324). The spatial notion of place as defining situations is reduced in significance by communications technologies and instead the social context of the interaction becomes an important characteristic of the setting.

Layered space

This has particularly strong resonances for our perception and action in urban public space. The social synthesis between the space of places and the space of flows is realized in public space (Castells 2004, 91). Public spaces or territories have a temporary quality and an individual has free access and occupancy rights (Altman 1975, 118). In everyday experience, they are often viewed as the 'in-between' spaces of the city; streets, parks, and transit routes. As they become increasingly densely interwoven with communications technologies, these everyday public spaces are transformed. A typical urban street is now wirelessly connected through a proliferating array of media, and a similarly wide set of practices associated with the interaction with such media is developing.

The consequence of communications technologies in urban settings is that multiple social realities can occur in one place. The same physical space may be caught within the domain of two different social occasions. The social situations that occur in these overlapping behavior settings support gatherings that possess a special characteristic in that they exist on more than one social level. The possibility that the same physical space can come to be used as a setting for more than one social occasion is regularly recognized. Thus in the case of public streets, there is a tendency in western society to define these places as the scene of overriding social occasion to which other occasions should be subordinated (Goffman 1963, 20). For example, presence in public space and interaction has traditionally been equated with face-to-face contact. Yet presence in public space as mediated by new technologies has a different type of aesthetic, no longer dominated by visual access but by informational access. The features and structure of the interaction is enabled by a connection, which is not necessarily achieved through physical movement from one location to another. As such, everyday actions and behaviors no longer belong to particular places, and are now multiplexed and overlaid; there now exists the possibility to switch rapidly from one activity to another while remaining in the same place, so we end up using the same place in many different ways. On one hand, this gives rise to confusion, and ambiguous and contested zones emerge

(Mitchell 1995, 101), where the multiple and overlapping behaviors created create disparate, fragmented, and discontinuous spatial references. On the other hand, we can consider space as a field of interaction, composed of intersections of mobile elements it is in a sense actuated by the ensemble of movements deployed within it (de Certeau 1984, 117). In this case space is perceived as practiced place rather than a fixed and intransitive bounded entity, and as such emerging practices can only serve to enhance the richness of our spatial experience.

Nodes and networks

As everyday public space becomes increasingly layered, the nature of spatial identity in these environments is changed. But communications networks tend to be largely invisible and silent, or at most relatively hard to discern; most weave unseen through the fabric of urban spaces, using very little space (Graham and Marvin 1996, 50). These networks bind together places in many different spatial and temporal positions in the form of real time networks. The result is that there is a general tendency for people to ignore or even deny the effects of the invisible environments of media simply because they are invisible.

The immateriality of communications networks is not just a superficial outcome of the technology infrastructure; it is fundamentally intrinsic to the nature of data transmission in such networks. This is in part because such information transfer is achieved through what are termed 'packet networks'. When information is transmitted in a communications network, a process occurs where the original data is divided up into uniform sized parcels of bits, called packets. In preparing data to be sent in the network, each packet is labeled with a header stating from which message it was drawn, its position in the message, and its destination. Each individual packet is then sent through any communications route that has capacity, so that the original data is literally totally dispersed in the network, and only realized as a whole again when it is reassembled upon reaching its destination (Pool 1990, 33). At each end of the network connection a node provides the sites of arrival and departure for the data, where temporary data may also be further processed or recorded onto memory. Consequently, one can consider the nature of information flow as enabled only through its own fragmentation, such that it is not possible to conceive of the information as sustaining any materiality during transmission. Whilst in transit the content and form of information is thus everywhere and nowhere; in fact, it can only be tangibly realized at the node. In wireless networks the data is not even confined to a cable linking two nodes, but is instead literally transmitted through the air at frequencies or wavelengths close to the speed of light. These abstract material characteristics of communications technologies mean that it is both conceptually and practically complex to form adequate perceptual parallels with existing concrete and imaginable concepts of space.

Imageability and invisibility

Our perception and action in space is in part made possible by our ability to act on mental models of the space and our position in it, whether physical or social. The question then arises as how we perceive the spaces of communications media in the city if we can neither see, hear, nor touch them, nor model their structure on existing bounded spatial concepts. It would seem that the layering of digital and physical space enables us to experience some sort of intertwining of experience, which is subsequently conceptualized. As with mental maps of urban spaces, images of the abstract topologies of communications networks and electronic spaces need to have emotional and subjective information about the qualities of the electronic place found, as well as what is where within the complex and intertwined web of physical spaces (Graham and Marvin 1996, 122). However it seems that the frameworks of communications media are being mapped too carelessly onto the spatial structures of the city, in part because the dilemma exists of how to give such media spatial and visual form. The lack of coherent visual or spatial identity indicates that such nodal points and networks problematizes the creation of meaningful internal or mental representations. Yet wireless communication technologies are becoming extremely dense in urban settings; each square meter of the city is increasingly populated by nodes, whether public or private, so that their presence cannot be denied in the spatial city. But the manner in which the city is traditionally perceived in visual terms has implications for the image of the city as this has by its own definition an inherently visual form. If these nodes, however dense, are not perceived in visual or spatial terms, then they will not enter in the consciousness as an aspect of the imageability of the city. If the overlay of the space of places and Castells' space of flows is working on parallel but mutually incoherent layers, this means that cities are becoming invisible to us in certain important ways.

Envisaging urban nodes

In order to try to understand more clearly some of the characteristics of the emerging spaces of mobile technologies, the series of images that follows will investigate the nature of the visual presence of a series of WiFi nodes in urban public space. The images seek specifically to explore the visual aesthetic of these nodes and to look at the characteristics of the layered public space created in their sphere. In order to deal with the condition more authentically the images are created through a variation of the practice known as 'wardriving'.[6] This involves traveling through the city with specialist equipment for detecting WiFi node locations. In this particular study, a webcam was connected to a laptop, which was programmed to record images when a node was detected. Images were subsequently captured over a period of sixty seconds so as to reflect the changing temporal nature of the condition. The intention of this method of image capture is to record more authentically the nature of the visual and

---

6   Wardriving is the practice of detecting and mapping wireless access points.

aesthetic qualities of the node that is perceived, as it were, from the viewpoint of the technology itself.

Currently, many wireless internet nodes are protected by secure encryption, which makes the WiFi network only accessible to the owner or to those authorized by the owner. This study takes place in London, UK where, as in many large western cities, a series of public resources have been established which seek not only to establish but also map the sites of wireless internet access. The images that follow draw on this resource and focus specifically on nodes that have been intentionally made public by their owners. Although these WiFi nodes are typically used for wireless internet access in a physically enclosed space, the hertzian signals from these nodes often spill out from private spaces into public. The information flow ignores the material thresholds of walls and doors, with the consequence that the physical extent or territory of the signal typically extends beyond traditional physically bounded notions of space.

Figure 10.1 Boundless.five
Source: Author.

The first node, shown in Figure 10.1, is located in Deptford, south-east London, and forms part of a larger community project entitled 'boundless,' which provides free WiFi access to citizens as part of a nodal network. These projects create new types of public space, characterized not by visible or physical access such as traditional public gathering spaces of parks or street corners, but instead by information access. In these spaces the entrance, provided by the node, is to non-physical territories.

The significance of such access is underlined when it is ceases to exist, and the character of the physical space is subsequently transformed. The second image (Figure 10.2) investigates the site of the London's first public wireless internet project in Clink Street, located on the south bank of the River Thames. The project was disbanded in the late nineties when a rise in property prices forced the co-operative responsible for the project out of their valuable waterside converted warehouse offices. The site is now occupied by a Starbucks café offering only commercial wireless internet access.

Figure 10.2 belkin 54g
Source: Author.

The buildings along the cobbled street have ceased to be a gathering point or a site of coming together where doors were welcomingly left open not just in terms of information access but also social interaction. It has instead assumed a characteristic of bounded space, and as such the pedestrian flow along the adjacent street, whilst ceaseless, no longer has any opportunity to pause en route. The potential for social interaction and thus an important quality of the place is effectively erased, enduring only as a memory or trace of that which once existed.

Figure 10.3 Thamesonline
Source: Author.

In contrast, the site of the third node in Figure 10.3 provides both a public space to pause briefly and a corresponding open WiFi node. Located within Neal's Yard, a courtyard surrounded by health-food shops and therapy rooms, which in its central location provides a rare opportunity for meeting without the need to for some form of purchase. It is here that the digital space of the node and the social space of the city seem to complement one another most fully. The transitory nature of visits in the courtyard, with visitors recurrently entering and leaving from appointments, balances alongside the space of flows of the network, with its fluid forming and breaking of linkages enabled centered on the node.

Figure 10.4 wh wireless
Source: Author.

Located nearby is the fourth node, shown in Figure 10.4, which is characterized by large gatherings of people, mainly tourists or visitors, but the social interaction is more transitory and never realized as an encounter, for it is too fleeting and superficial. The existing model of access and as site of interaction is exemplified here, but there is almost no availability of public WiFi nodes reflecting a public space that fails to stimulate meaningful interaction. Here the fluid crowds form and disperse, but without exchange or communication, with the experience often remaining purely as a visual encounter with the space.

Figure 10.5 xyzzy
Source: Author.

   In order to instantiate a node in a location it must be named or labeled with a tag. Interestingly in all the sites in the study the node names rarely any relation to the static physical location. This is despite the fact that both the hardware and signals from such nodes have a very distinct spatial extent and position. For instance the node in Figure 10.5, though located in the particularly distinctive location of Greenwich covered market in south London, is denoted by the un-descriptive label of 'xyzzy'. Since conventionally it is implicit that space is claimed by the act of naming it, this emphasizes the extent to which the nodes are not considered primarily in spatial terms. Instead the node references either the modem hardware that enables the WiFi node or the name of the network, both parts of the technology infrastructure. Indeed the very vagueness of the word 'node' indicates the loss of a language for naming environmental value (Sennett, in Carter *et al.* 1993, 319). The identity of the node is not perceived as delineating spatial territory or having temporal qualities, whether physical or digital. Nodes are understood more along the metaphor of switches, which simply establish and break linkages. As such they equate with access to information, where the accessibility of information flows is replacing the visual and spatial quality of access of sight and of body. In this sense, the important notion of visibility in the city as equating with physical and social access is being transformed into access to information.

Summary

We live, act, and orient ourselves in a spatial world that is richly and profoundly differentiated into places. They are sources of security and identity and they qualify our perception and actions. Yet we do not perceive the spatial world through our senses alone, but engage in many strategies to order to make the spatial world knowable. The resulting mental construct is an environmental image; a highly personalized model of the external world that includes physical features and qualities. However, our essentially spatial perspective on the world is called into question with mobile and wireless technologies, a form of ubiquitous computing where the focus is not on the technology itself but rather on what it is enabling. The physical world comes to be considered as part of the space of the digital interaction. Yet the converging of physical and digital space gives rise to a series of significant transformations in perception and action in social situations. The nature of this experience is most concentrated in urban public space, where the virtually invisible quality of the nodes and networks of communications technologies create multiple and sometimes inconsistent layers of physical and digital space. The physical 'glue' holding space together is thus transformed, such that instead of thinking of specific places with boundaries around, they can be imagined concurrently as articulated flows in networks of social encounters and situations. These more fluid and abstract notions of space interrupt our mental images of space since physical form and visual appearance have conventionally shaped our perception in the spatial city. As such the nodes and networks are coming to be considered along the lines of the social interaction that they facilitate, with the pattern of breaks and linkages to the invisible flow of communication mapped densely over the space of places.

References

Altman, I. (1975), *The Environment and Social Behavior* (California: Wadsworth).

Carter, E. *et al.* (1993), *Space and Place: Theories of Identity and Location* (London: Lawrence and Wishart).

Castells, M. (2004), 'Space of Flows, Space of Places: Materials for a Theory of Urbanism in the Information Age', in Graham, S. (ed.).

de Certeau, M. (1984), *The Practice of Everyday Life* (London: University of California Press).

Downs, M. and Stea, D. (eds) (1973), *Image and Environment, Cognitive Mapping and Spatial Behavior* (Chicago: Aldine).

Goffman, E. (1963), *Behavior in Public Places; Notes on the Social Occasion of Gatherings* (New York: The Free Press).

Graham, S. (ed.) (2004), *The Cybercities Reader* (London: Routledge).

Graham, S. and Marvin, S. (1996), *Telecommunications and the City: Electronic Spaces, Urban Places* (London: Routledge).

Lynch, K. (1960), *The Image of the City* (Cambridge Mass: MIT Press).

Meyrowitz, J. (1986), *No Sense of Place: The Impact of the Electronic Media on*

Social Behaviour (USA: Oxford).

Mitchell, W. (1995), *City of Bits; Space, Place and the Infobahn* (Cambridge Mass: MIT Press).

Pool, I. de S. (1990), *Technologies without Boundaries: On Telecommunications in a Global Age* (Cambridge Mass: Harvard University Press).

Relph, E. (1976), *Place and Placelessness* (London: Pion).

Virilio, P. (1997), *Open Sky* (London: Verso).

Weiser, M. (1994), 'The Computer for the Twenty First Century', *Scientific American* 265:3, 94–104.

Chapter 11

Working with the Visual

Lars Frers and Lars Meier

Figure 11.1 Encountering Urban Places
Source: Authors of this volume.

An idyll haunted by a potential encounter with the other, managing to move a family down a railway platform, the lure of a lush siren in neon, creating a Minibar on Ankara's sidewalks, the idea of protest and revolution, Indian restaurants in Rome, bankers hurrying along the sidewalk of the City of London, someone crossing the border between observer and guest, and ghost-like figures walking along an empty street – these pictures illustrate arguments made in this volume, serve to analyze performances in the visual and material realm of the city, confront us with provocations and struggles, and challenge our ways of seeing and understanding urban everyday life and the encounters it produces. In the following, we will discuss the ways in which images are used in this volume. Focusing on the pictures and text present in this volume, we want to contemplate the different shades of the wide spectrum that is brought into view through the implementation of visual entities in a book on contemporary urban life.

Doing this, we will both pay attention to the pictures that are presented – their aesthetics and what they display – and to the way they are embedded in the text – the text that is usually considered to be the sole heart of the academic enterprise. We will not discuss most of the intricate and important technical aspects of producing the pictures, although it has great impact on what can actually be seen here. The choice of lens and the specific distortion that goes along with it, the range of focus, the use of zooms, the duration of exposure, the way light is used, and the vast array of modifications and alterations made possible by digital editing of the pictures will not be discussed here.[1] Instead, we want to concentrate on the phenomenology of the picture, its relation to text, and on some of the social processes that go along with using pictures in the social sciences.

Some of the peculiarities of the picture are related to its unclear epistemological status. The picture, and especially the photograph, can be regarded as being a more or less direct representation of the things that have been 'captured' by the act of producing the picture (be it making a quick sketch or clicking the release trigger on a digital camera). Frozen time, which can be used as proof or example. At the same time, the production of the picture is an artistic act, a creation of something new, something with specific qualities, that can be regarded as mundane or sublime, as professional or amateurish, intriguing or boring. Accordingly, the way a picture is seen may change dramatically according to whom is perceiving and judging it. 'Reading the picture' is a task of its own, and actually it is a task that is quite different to reading a text; 'experiencing the picture' or 'living it' might be more fitting descriptions of what happens when one is looking at a picture. In this context the last peculiarity of these visual entities becomes relevant: what is seen and how it is experienced changes according to the circumstances of seeing the picture. Both the situation of the viewer and the arrangement of the picture in relation to its surroundings can make enormous differences. Compared to text, especially the linear text of printed publications, pictures harbor a specific openness. This is not to say that text is not open too – it can also be produced, arranged, and read in many different ways. However, especially in the academic world, the ways in which texts are read and produced are highly standardized, subject to the uniforming process of peer review and a hierarchizing culture of academic reputation, whereas pictures are more of a border phenomenon, something that is present, but not (yet) thoroughly regulated and therefore open to many different uses. Additionally, because of its inherent aesthetic or perceptual qualities, seeing a picture is not a linear and uniform

---

1   A classic text on photography in anthropology is *Visual Anthropology* by Collier and Collier (1986). Emmison and Smith (2000), Goodwin (2000), Rose (2001), and Kanstrup (2002) discuss visual methods and methodologies, and the use of photography in social science. See Friday (2002) for a philosophical discussion on the aesthetics of photography.

experience. Many pictures, and most of those that are present in this volume, offer a myriad of details that can be looked at and scrutinized. What will be the first thing that one sees, how the discovery proceeds, if and when will it produce astonishment, joy, or dismay – this is not clear and it is difficult to regulate. In the remainder of this concluding chapter we will show how the authors of this volume dealt with these peculiarities of the visual in their individual chapters.

The visual as illustration

In spite of the unpredictabilities of how a picture is seen and interpreted, it lends itself to be used as an illustration for an argument or as a representation of something that exists in the real world, something that could have been experienced by the reader/ viewer too. It carries an implicit expectation, a hope that the reader will read the text, see the picture, and believe in the truth of the description that has been given. However, in this volume the specific kinds of representation offered by the printed photographs is being put into focus. Jerry Krase in his chapter on ethnic vernacular landscapes in Rome argues that the evidence that is produced by the works of visual sociology can work as an antidote to the problems faced by statistics on the presence of aliens in a given population. He gathers the many representations of ethnicity that are displayed in the streets of cities and presents these different displays to the readers, directing their attention the ways in which the undocumented aliens too become visible for those that walk the streets of a metropolis like Rome or New York. Martina Löw, Lars Frers, and Lars Meier also use photographs as representations of their own subjective experiences: the surprise of seeing an advertisements for a brothel in Vienna's airport; the ways in which stepping out of a terminal can make one stop, throw off restricting envelopes, and look at a new scenery; and the interest in discovering an exciting and challenging foreign environment like Brixton. Łukasz Stanek in turn shows simulations, scenes in which people encounter a simulated environment or even their own past as a simulation. Other aspects are not as easily represented in a photograph. Katharine Willis tackles the invisible; using multiple exposures and digitally editing her photographs, she shows that something is there that can normally not be seen, thus representing an experience that is missing.

Zeuler Lima and Vera Pallamin chose a different route for representing the role played by the void below the museum that has been designed by Lina Bo Bardi – after first considering the use of photographs to show the place and its uses, they reconsidered what they wanted to show the readers and finally decided to produce their own illustrations, drawn by Zeuler Lima. Drawings and painting usually have a greater degree of abstraction from the real world than a photograph; they show specific aspects of what can be perceived. This has the advantage that the illustration can concentrate on those aspects that are deemed relevant. As passionate bird watchers know, well done illustrations make the identification of birds much easier than photographs – the illustrators can concentrate on representing the decisive aspects that allow differentiating one species from another, additional information (the 'excess of fact' as Helen Liggett puts it – we will get to that concept later) can be left out, since it would only distract from the purpose at hand. Another advantage of the drawing or painting is that it does not need a 'real' referent – it can represent imaginations, ideas, or ideals. Zeuler Lima and Vera Pallamin can therefore direct the attention of their readers/viewers to the aspects that they want to present. Of course, it is still no guarantee that the aspects are interpreted in the way they are thought or intended to be.

So far, we have talked about the individual picture as a representation. However, in many of the chapters in this volume the photos, video stills, or illustrations offer themselves to be read as sequences of pictures, telling a story or several stories that run parallel to the text. Helen Liggett describes the way she arranges photographs in her chapter:

> [...] photographs are presented in carefully constructed series in which the force of the connections among the images produce further meaning than that found in the individual images. Arranged without text or captions the sequence is a visual performance. [...] In my use of photographic sequence I continue to use images as a language, to use internal elements to cite each other and to build meaning by juxtaposition. In addition, images relate to the text as well as produce a parallel performance.

> The sequence in this chapter moves from geometry to gesture. This is analogous to the arguments in the text from abstract representations of space to concrete practice. (Chapter Two)

The illustrations in the chapter of Zeuler Lima and Vera Pallamin can be read as a comic strip, telling the story of a place in which the 'redistributing the sensible' establishes a location for practices of dissent.

> As many of the illustrations in this article show, banners, posters, costumes, art works, temporary installations, flags, musical instruments, shields, human barricades are just a few of the many tools used to accentuate the many voices and bodies to protest, celebrate and negotiate common values and social relationships. (Chapter Six)

Similarly, though with the use of long-exposure photographs, Deniz Altay lets the pictures tell a story about the fleeting nature of the practice of creating Minibars. Can Altay has arranged his exhibition of photographs as a slideshow, evoking a sense of the gap that is searched for and filled by the participants of Minibars. In all of these cases, the pictures in their sequentiality tell their own stories, stories that are related to the text, supplementing it, but also providing an experience that is unique, that offers an aesthetic understanding, an experience of its own (or a 'parallel performance' as Helen Liggett puts it) which cannot be provided by the reading of a text.

In Lars Frers' chapter, the video stills are arranged in temporal order, following the path through time and space that has been taken during the passage through Kiel's main railway station. Below each of the images, a marker on a time scale shows where in the sequence the video still is located. In this case the order of the pictures, their sequentiality, is intended quite directly as a representation of a sequentiality that unfolds itself in observable everyday actions. In accordance with ethnomethodological approaches, what can be seen is taken as exactly that: things that can be seen and that are actively displayed by actors, and things to which actors align themselves, displaying this alignment (or their refusal of aligning themselves) to their surroundings.

Of course, using images as representations always remains a problematic endeavor. It cannot be guaranteed that they haven't been tampered with, the circumstances under which they have been taken are unknown, and it is quite unclear if they are actually representative of what they supposedly represent: depending on time and weather, a public place may seem deserted and void even though it usually is lively and full of people; depending on what one puts into focus and how, a place may seem to be homogenous, threatening, or peaceful. In this regard, an image does not speak for its referent and if it serves to represent the character of a place giving some information regarding the context of the picture and its production would help its viewers to judge and contextualize in turn what they are seeing – even if this is certainly no safeguard to congruency between the picture and its referent.

The visual as analysis

We have talked about the ways in which images have been used as more or less direct representations of aspects of the real world, and we have seen that some of the chapters in this volume tell their stories through their interrelations, their sequences and through the flow of emotions that one feels when going from one part of the sequence to the next. However, another way of implementing the visual is to scrutinize it closely, taking it apart to show something that usually is overlooked because it is too small, passes too quickly, or because one would usually be too entangled in a situation to be able to stand back and analyze what one sees. Lars Frers follows an ethnomethodological approach, recording sequences of action and then analyzing their components in detail to show how they are related to each other and to show how people through their real-time efforts (re)create social and also visual order around them. To this end he freezes situations that follow each other, inspects what people experience in these situations, and how they proceed to move on from there. Jerry Krase looks at the semiotics of the visual, how people symbolize their identity and culture in their surroundings. In his photos he shows how they compete for representation and visual presence in urban spaces, producing evidence that is necessary for understanding social processes as they are seen and experienced by the inhabitants of shared spaces. Martina Löw in turn tells us about situations that are laden with anxiety and hidden rules; her pictures – and her very illustrative descriptions – evoke a sense of how the visual governs interactions in the realm of seduction, sex, and commerce. The way an event like choosing which woman should be one's companion is staged, the way lust is symbolized, and the ways in which the workings of the sex business are hidden from the view of outsiders are analyzed by a careful selection and close inspection of what can be seen in the red light world.

The visual as confrontation

The photos and illustrations in this volume show objects and people, they tell stories, illustrate arguments, capture fleeting moments and offer raw material for social scientific analysis. But they can be much more than that; they can be tough confrontations with what we usually keep out of our sight, because it makes us uncomfortable or because it would stir us out of our everyday routines. In this regard, good images are like good art: they evoke emotions that tell us about life and make us think about how life is and how it could be; about the good, the bad, and the ugly.

Still, before we involve ourselves more intimately with the aesthetics of the pictures and what they show us, a sociologically informed step back will be taken. The position to which we step back has a solid foundation, built by Pierre Bourdieu. Taking his perspective on art, the realm of taste, and judgement reveals that the perception of art and its discontents is always intertwined with matters of distinction (Bourdieu 1984). Martina Löw describes how different social milieus are addressed by visual clues that are displayed by brothels catering to their specific customers. A variation on the theme of distinction is performed in Nowa Huta, where the simulation of Nowa Huta's communist past is used to produce a distance to the past of this exemplary 'socialist city' and its inhabitants. In the course of this distancing by means of simulation, the inhabitants of Nowa Huta are displayed as being inferior. As Łukasz Stanek tells us, this specific way of exposing them and their past makes them feel like 'apes in the zoo', the scorned and primitive other, the past that a post-communist society has left behind, like evolution has left behind the species of the great apes, which is now falling pray to progress.

Distinction can also be a game of provocations. Some of the pictures in this volume have the potential to provoke. Again, the open display of sexuality may provoke those who feel that prostitution is an immoral business and that the sex business has no place in the public realm – exposing a nipple, even if it is a neon nipple, crosses the lines of what many would consider decency. In her chapter on the Minibar, Deniz Altay shows both sides of the provocation – on the one hand we have young men and women mingling freely on the streets of Ankara, seemingly not caring much about the expectations of neighbors and police, pouring some substance, possibly a drug, into their self-mixed drinks, while on the other hand we have fences with stake-like ends, placed to defend and fortify a space; a material provocation to those that define the same space as public and open to all, accordingly, parts of the fence are bent, they have been vandalized by those that have been declared to be trespassers and vandals.

Provocations are also part of the struggles and contests that cross life in the city. Reading this volume, we are being confronted with many different struggles. These struggles are centered around having a place in the urban landscape. In case of the immigrants that are the object of Jerry Krase's study, the struggle is about creating a place to define and live an ethnic identity in today's multi-ethnic metropolitan cities – different ethnic representations compete which each other, all present their own symbols, language and practices in the streets. Zeuler Lima and Vera Pallamin are focussing on explicitly political struggles – clashes with police forces and brandished flags in a place of central importance, imbued with a history of competing demands put forth by the bourgeoisie, by artists, by politicians, and by business; the use and design of the space below and around the museum on the Terraço do Trianon is politically charged:

> [...] politics emerge out of the need of the excluded to affirm their presence and to have their identity recognized. This process ties political practice with symbolic representation. The convergence between aesthetics and politics provides an important insight into the fleeting meaning and social and physical constituency of urban spaces such as Terraço do Trianon. This approach to how aesthetics are politicized reveals how certain conditions of perception and expression are included or excluded in democratic cultural and social relations. (Chapter Six)

These struggles about what Lefebvre calls the 'right to the city' (Lefebvre 1996) are discussed in many of the contributions to this volume. In our everyday lives, these struggles take place in our encounters with others present in the same places. The photos made by Helen Liggett offer a sense of what the potentials of non-instrumental encounters are, how people's practices can assemble and produce moments and spaces that counter the oppressive force of abstract representations of space, which are invading everyday life. As Lars Frers puts it, the logic of envelopment that is produced in interaction with the design of urban places accompanies this struggle between openness and closure, between spontaneity and efficiency, and between risk and control.

Katharine Willis and Lars Meier both have set themselves on the difficult path of confronting the readers/viewers of their chapters with what is not visible. The pictures of Katharine Willis try to fill the missing experience of the ether – something that generations have been searching for in vain. The ether, the medium that carries electromagnetic waves, does not exist. Yet, the waves exist, and they impact our practices in the city in many ways. Her pictures confront us with the invisible, giving occasion for reflection on a life in which we walk through layers of communication networks seemingly unaffected, though permeated by packeted data signals. Lars Meier deals with another problem that is generated by the absence of something that is an intrinsic part of our modern way of living – the unseen workers that keep the heart of the world's economy pumping. He confronts the narrations of bankers with what he saw and photographed in those times in which the business people flow out of the City and later he also confronts the tell-tale accounts of the bankers with the seeming normality of Brixton.

The visual that is assembled in this volume harbors the potential to show how distinction is achieved, the photos and images may provoke, and they confront us with the struggles and risks that are part of the richness of urban life. The illustrations and photographs raise images that may be neglected, overlooked, invisible, or unpleasant – they show us urban life in many guises, in different times, and on different continents, reminding us of what makes urban places an exciting and important subject of an engaged scientific study.

Challenges of the visual

So far, we have mostly treated the ways in which the photos and illustrations in this volume are presented to their viewers and how they are used in relation to the text; we have not yet given much account of the challenges that one faces during the production and implementation of the visual. One of the most obvious problems for those who use a camera (both photo or video) is how to treat their objects. Often, using the camera is regarded as an intrusion. People are rightly suspicious of what is happening and the number of pictures in which one can see people throwing skeptical looks into the direction of the camera and its wielder is accordingly large. In this context, we will only touch on this topic to outline some of the hazards and potential ways around them. The most pleasant and rewarding way is probably the most time-consuming way too: getting to know the people one wants to photographs or videotape, earning their trust, and becoming a part of their routine, so that they know what is happening, why one is interested in them, and what might actually be done with pictures of them and what they do. Of course, not all settings allow for such an approach. It would be impossible to get to know the random people that walk through a major railway station and it would interrupt their routines even more if one would ask for permission before or after taking a photograph. In these cases, respect for the intimacy of the photographed or filmed subjects is of crucial importance – especially if one does not get explicit consent for taking pictures of people, one should very much consider how to treat them in a way that protects their privacy. The zoom of a camera is an incredible tool, and it enables the person wielding the camera to get much closer to a person that most would allow a stranger to come. Accordingly, one has to consider carefully if and when such an invasion would be appropriate and if and under what circumstances it actually could be legitimately pursued. Sometimes, consent is implicit or displayed by minor gestures. If people notice the photographer, and do not look annoyed, or walk out of focus, instead just ignoring the camera or even making small gestures to check if their looks are fine, some kind of implicit agreement has been reached. In some countries and/or academic institutions there are explicit and often strict guidelines regarding these ethics of research; in others these decisions are being left to the individual researcher – still, considering these issues is something that is a permanent aspect of work in the field. Regardless of legal regulations, it is an intimate and difficult part of the practice of observing and recording the activities of those that get into the focus of research.

Other decisions have to be made too. One concerns the question in how far taking a picture should be staged and if this kind of staging has to be communicated to the reader/viewer. Depending on the kind of representation or effect that the picture should have, one has to take this into account. If a picture should characterize a place, for example, it would add much to the adequacy of this representation if the conditions under which the picture has been produced are stated: when has a picture been taken; has the photographer made specific efforts to produce this picture; why was it necessary to make these efforts? This is not to say that the flow of an argument or the flow of a story told by images has to be interrupted by listing the conditions and circumstances of its production. However, pondering when and how this is done makes the argument stronger, either by protecting it against doubt or by clearly demarkation its – limited – validity. Similarly thinking about the huge amount of pictures that don't find their way into a finished book or article is an enlightening way of reflecting on the stories we tell. Why have all these other pictures been left out? Would they tell a different story? Often, an argument gets only stronger if it anticipates and explicitly deals with counter arguments that may be raised by those who read and view the text and the images skeptically.

In addition, reflecting about the situation and perspective of possible readers might also enhance the effect that is achieved with photographs and illustrations. To us it seems to be the case much too often that those who make the pictures – having thought about which of them they want to have printed, having dealt with their size, quality, and content – forget that what they see on these pictures might not at all be clear or obvious to others who look at the picture. Some readers/viewers might just glance over the pictures if what can be seen on them is not pointed out more explicitly. 'Reading' pictures is a skill that can be learned – encouraging one's readers to do so would be one way of helping them learn this skill, giving them some pointers as to where they should start might also be a good idea. Depending on the kinds of pictures one uses it might also be relevant to think about possible color blindness and about reduced vision. Details that are too tiny to discern or effects that base purely on green-red contrasts might get lost for certain viewers. Investing some thought and time into the complexity of the pictures that people encounter when reading/viewing an article or book helps to reconstruct the phenomenology or experience of reading – keeping the substantial differences between reading a linear, printed text, reading a hyper text, looking at a photo or illustration, looking at a sequence of images, or watching a video in mind can lead to one's work being even more accessible and convincing.

One more challenge has to be faced by those willing to invest time and thought into the visual. Most of the photographs, video stills, and illustrations in this volume have been produced by the authors themselves – one of the main reasons for this is the fact that copyright issues make the use of pictures that have not been produced by an author her or himself or a by a friend or relative a difficult and sometimes frustrating endeavor. Several of the contributors to this volume dropped pictures because getting permission to use them either seemed to complicated or daunting or because it would be too expensive. From our perspective this is a big problem, and one that can got worse over the course of the last years in which many of the major photo archives have been acquired by private companies that use them to produce profit. One of the ways to counter this development is to make the pictures one takes available to the public – Jerry Krase in particular is very generous in this regard, trying to make access to his huge archive of photographs easy and distributing his pictures freely to those who ask for them; another way to counter this development is to use the internet as a resource and to contribute to pools like the Wikimedia Commons[2] or the Creative Commons,[3] which allow for different licenses regulating public and commercial use of the content one produces.

Only visual?

Finally, we want to briefly discuss some limits of the visual. Both Lars Meier and Katharine Willis argue that the distance that is kept by the sense of sight makes perspectives and encounters that rely solely on the gaze are lacking – the view of the city as a landscape ignores the corporality of living in the city, and only transitory contact or communication is established between those who rush through Covent Garden. However, the visual can still evoke a sense of the concrete materiality that is experienced by those that encounter urban places. Martina Löw approaches this distanced situation from the other side, showing how arranging the gaze creates hierarchies: when the women working in a brothel are called forth by the barmaid, telling them to show themselves for the customer, the customer is put into a position of power and the women's bodies become arranged like a picture that his eyes are free to roam over, moving the customer from a position of insecurity to a position that gives the powers of choice. Because of the delicacy of the subject matter, she is creating this image through her text – taking a photograph would both break the fragile setting and invade a space that is all about creating a sense of protected pricacy.

Though relying on the visual, the photos of Helen Liggett tell stories that focus very much on the bodies, their gestures, and their relation to each other. Lars Frers also uses photographs to make corporeal arrangements sensible to the viewers, trying to show how people align their posture and movements to their material and social surroundings. Nonetheless, not all of these bodily aspects or urban encounters can be visualized easily in pictures – sometimes it is just not possible to have photos at hand that show the relevant configurations that need to be analyzed; sometimes the situation does not allow recording images, as in the example of Martina Löw's study of the brothel. In these cases text can very well make relations tangible – one of the most sensually impressive examples in this volume is given by Łukasz Stanek: the 'mythical mud' of Nowa Huta through which the visitor of a exhibition could be walking. Walking or paddling through the mud is an experience that involves all senses: sight, smell, hearing, and, of course, touch and movement. Thus, both the text and the visual evidence given by photos and illustrations can evoke experiences that are not limited to the sense of sight, giving access to those aspects of experience

---

2   http://commons.wikimedia.org/
3   http://creativecommons.org/

that are not directly visible. Still, it is difficult to work against the sensual reduction that happens if one is concentrating on the visual alone. Even in pictures, the depth and the experiential horizon of one's gaze are lost. It is very hard if not impossible to reproduce colors in a faithful way, since the perception of color always happens in a context of different lighting around the person that sees. In addition, the color range of printed pictures is much reduced when compared to the colors we can see in our everyday surroundings. Of course, it is lost practically completely in grayscale pictures like those printed in this volume.

In spite of all of these difficulties with employing and reproducing the visual as the only 'sensual bonus' to the text offered in this volume, we hope to have made life in the city, to have made encounters with its people and its places, more tangible to you. As Helen Liggett puts it, the photos offer an 'excess of fact', leaving room for the viewers to be productive themselves:

> If making photographs is not about capturing an object, but about making a space; then making good photographs means that photographic space always contains some element to be discovered. In successful sequences the connections are to be discovered and enjoyed by the viewers. (Chapter Two)

In this sense, we hope that the visual and textual contributions in this volume have awoken a desire to be involved in the life of the city, to discover its many different sides, and to be open to the many opportunities offered by urban encounters.

References

Bourdieu, P. (1984), *Distinction: A Social Critique of the Judgment of Taste* (Cambridge, Mass: Harvard University Press).

Collier, J., Jr. and Collier, M. (1986), *Visual Anthropology: Photography as a Research Method* (Albuquerque: University of New Mexico Press).

Emmison, M. and Smith, P. (2000), *Researching the Visual: Images, Objects, Contexts and Interactions in Social and Cultural Inquiry* (London: Sage).

Friday, J. (2002), *Aesthetics and Photography* (Aldershot: Ashgate).

Goodwin, C. (2000), 'Practices of Seeing: Visual Analysis: An Ethnomethodological Approach', in T.v. Leeuwen and C. Jewitt (eds).

Kanstrup, A.M. (2002), 'Picture the Practice: Using Photography to Explore Use of Technology within Teachers' Work Practices', *Forum Qualitative Research* 3:2.

Kofman, E. and Lebas, E. (eds) (1996), Henri Lefebvre: Writings on Cities (London: Basil Blackwell).

van Leeuwen, T. and Jewitt, C. (eds) (2001), *Handbook of Visual Analysis* (London: Sage).

Lefebvre, H. (1996), 'The Right to the City', in Kofman, E. and Lebas, E. (eds).

Rose, G. (2001), *Visual Methodologies: An Introduction to the Interpretation of Visual Materials* (London: Sage).

Index